OSAKA

A pocket guide to the city's best cultural hangouts, shops, bars and eateries

STEVE WIDE &
MICHELLE MACKINTOSH

Hardie Grant
TRAVEL

海

CONTENTS

梅生地
たこやき
しお
マヨ
酢
梅生地
たこ焼
梅生地たこ焼き
•そのまま
•うめしお
•ソースマヨ
•しおマヨ
•しょうゆマヨ
•チーズ
•ねぎポン
•たこせん
梅生地
SAPPORO
生ビール
ハイボール
チューハイ
カクテル
梅酒
営業

INTRODUCTION

Osaka is Japan's third biggest city – the brash, messy and always hungry cousin to the west of Tokyo and Yokohama. Osaka loves to have a laugh, to eat well and it definitely knows how to throw a party. It's a pop-colour, pop-culture trip where it's easy to get lost amongst the crowds. The elegant, sophisticated Japan of legend gives way to an untethered street-style, off-the-cuff city that lives by the seat of its collective pants.

Osaka invented street food and Love Hotels, it brought American street culture to Japan and its general love of all things pop culture makes it a perfect destination for lovers of good times. The city is the home of comedy and many of Japan's most revered comedic duos hail from here. Osaka has friendly locals and crowded shopping malls. It has both lurid neon and handmade signs, vintage clothing and vinyl, and the very latest in fashions, where big-name brands go head-to-head with young, brash upstarts. Osaka has coffee culture and family entertainment, but it's also home to one of the world's most thriving nightlife and band scenes. Surprisingly, in the mix is one of Japan's oldest and most revered temples.

Osaka Pocket Precincts is crammed with all the tips you'll need to shop, eat, drink and explore this frenetic city. We'll take you to all the major over-the-top streets and mad department stores, and then whisk you into the quieter neighbourhoods for tea and wagashi (Japanese sweets). We'll take you to the best indie areas and creative hangouts, escape into green spaces, take a beer or whisky tour, and marvel at some of the most amazing architecture in the world. All followed by an onsen (hot springs bath) or temple retreat in our detailed field trips.

Let us guide you to our favourite places, give you the best stay-up-late options and early morning activities. We'll show you where to shop, where to eat and what to see, the unmissable and the unexpected and, most importantly, how to have fun like an Osaka local.

Steve & Michelle

キリンビール

A PERFECT OSAKA DAY

Our perfect day in Osaka always starts at one of our favourite coffee haunts, **Takamura Wine and Coffee Roasters**, **Lilo Coffee Roasters** or **The Gut's Coffee**, before heading to **Kuromon Ichiba Market** for a seafood rice bowl topped with the morning's freshest catch. We take a quick train to **Osaka–Umeda station** to window-shop in the food hall of **Hankyu Department Store**, then duck downstairs into the cavernous station to have a delicious lunch of takoyaki (battered octopus dumplings) and an okonomiyaki (savoury omelette pancake) at **Takohachi Takoyaki**. After that, it's time for a bit of nature at **Minoo Park** to admire the beautiful garden, the bridge and the waterfall, and to have a soak in **Minoo Onsen Spa**. From here, we indulge in an art excursion to one of our favourite places, the **Shiba Ryotaro Memorial Museum**, a wonderfully atmospheric place, designed by Tadao Ando for one of Japan's favourite authors, with towering bookshelves and a simply stunning building. Next, Michelle will head over to Minamisenba precinct, stroll around looking at the tiny boutiques, then pop into **Wad Omotenashi** for green tea and wagashi (Japanese sweets). Meanwhile, Steve will hotfoot it to Amerikamura and Horie precinct and do a quick dive into **Time Bomb Records**, some vintage shopping, then meet up with Michelle via **King Kong Records.** An afternoon's shopping sees us in the indie stores in Nakazakicho precinct, popping into **Green Pepe**, **Two Elephants** and **Elulu by Jam**. After a quick coffee at **Haiku Coffee Roasters**, we go for a stroll and a shop along **Tenjinbashi-suji Shopping Street**. Then it's time for a cheeky drink amongst the standing bars of **Ura-Tenma** and **Chochin-dori**. Tired, we head to Fukushima precinct for dinner at an eatery in the backstreets around the Fukushima and Shin Fukushima train stations and finally, a late-night bar hop in the tiny network of bars inside the crumbling glamour of the **Misono Building** in Namba precinct. To soak it all up, Steve will slurp a restorative ramen at **Kinryu Ramen Dotonbori**.

POCKET TOP PICKS

COFFEE

Haiku Coffee Roasters, Nakazakicho ... 19

Takamura Wine and Coffee Roasters, Fukushima & Higobashi ... 34

Ibuki Coffee Kuromon ... 42

Lilo Coffee Roasters, Amerikamura, Horie & Nishishinsaibashi ... 84

The Gut's Coffee, Nakazakicho ... 19

OMIYAGE (SOUVENIRS)

Takohachi Takoyaki, Osaka–Umeda station ... 10

Kuidaore Taro pudding, Osaka–Umeda station ... 8

Uncle Rikuro Cheese Cake, Osaka–Umeda station ... 8

Pom Pom Purin pudding cafe, Osaka–Umeda station ... 8

Octopus (tako) keyrings, soft toys and more, Osaka–Umeda station ... 8

FOOD

Kogaryu Takoyaki, Amerikamura, Horie & Nishishinsaibashi ... 88

Ajinoya, Shinsaibashi & Namba ... 59

Kushikatsu street food, Shinsekai & Tennoji ... 117

Harukoma Honten Sushi, Tenma ... 107

Kuromon Ichiba Market, Nipponbashi & Den Den Town ... 41

DRINKING SPOTS

Uesugi Liquor Store drink machines, Shinsekai & Tennoji ... 116

Shin Umeda Shokudo Street, Osaka–Umeda station ... 7

Oui bar, Shinsaibashi & Namba ... 60

Misono Building, Shinsaibashi & Namba ... 61

Noon + Cafe, Nakazakicho ... 23

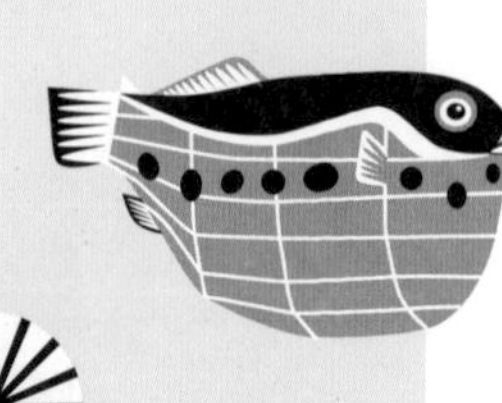

VIEWS

CULTURAL SPOTS

CRAZY SPOTS

RELAXING SPOTS

OSAKA OVERVIEW

HYOGO-KEN

OSAKA-FU

NISHIYODOGAWA-KU

PRECINCTS

FIELD TRIPS

FUKUSHIMA-

KONOHANA-KU

MINATO-KU

OSAKA

大阪市

TAISHO-KU

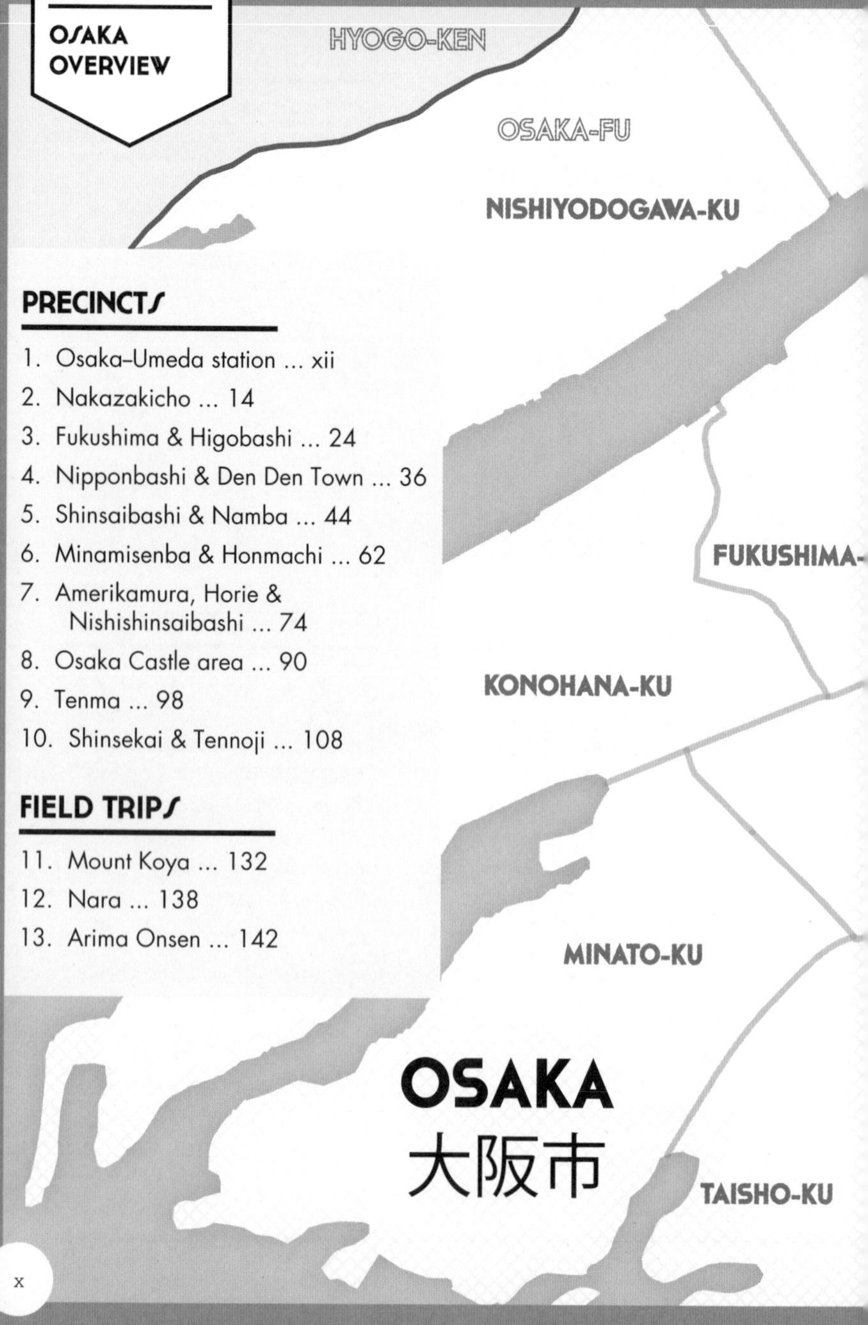

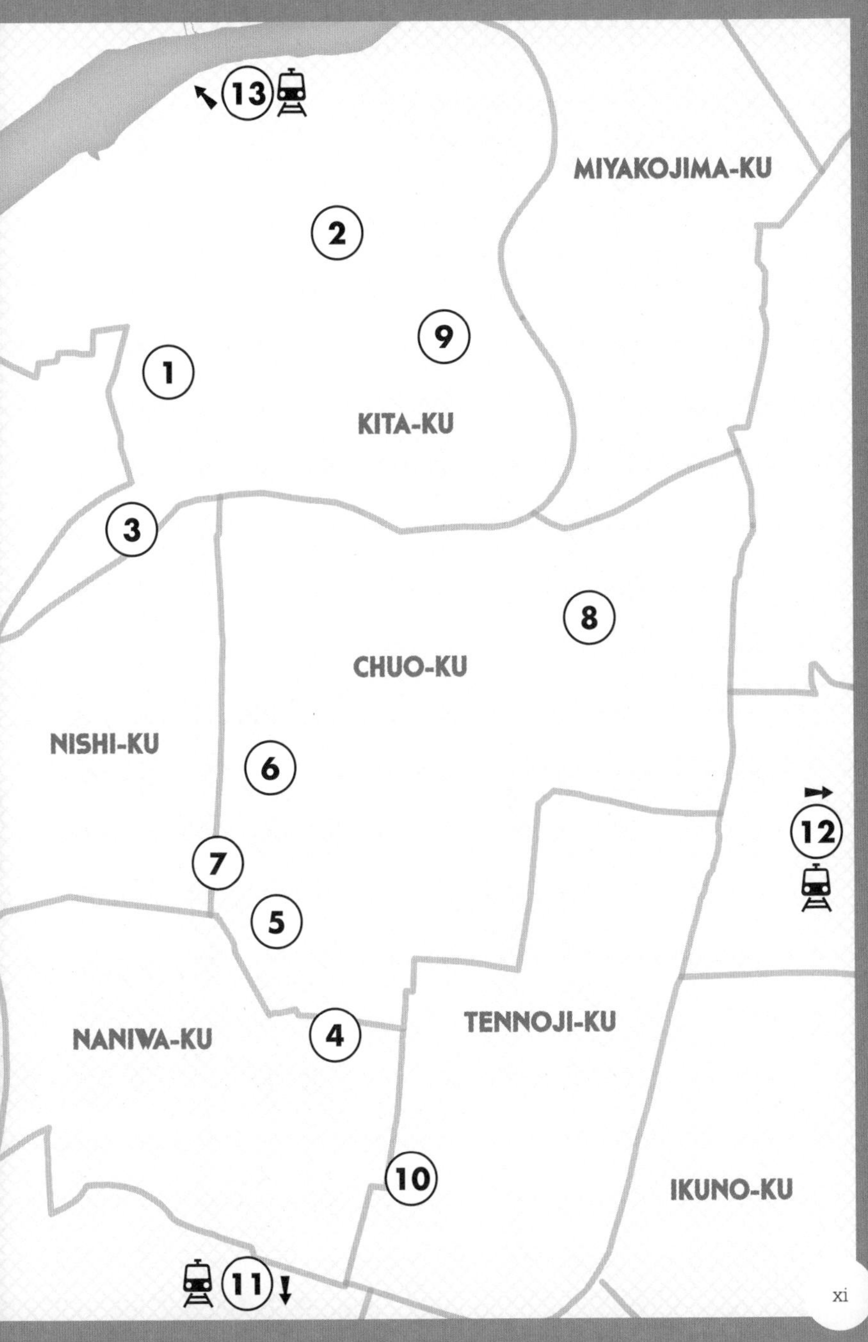
13
MIYAKOJIMA-KU
2
9
1
KITA-KU
3
8
CHUO-KU
NISHI-KU
6
12
7
5
4
TENNOJI-KU
NANIWA-KU
10
IKUNO-KU
11

OSAKA–UMEDA STATION

Somewhere along the way, Osaka and Umeda train stations married and became one – a long tunnel and shopping complex, and the central point in a vortex of shopping malls, eateries and Osaka landmarks. Three major train stations and six local satellite stations make sure that this central point tendrils out to many Osaka hotspots. Osaka is known for its food and the last thing the city would want is for you to go home empty-handed. The underground tunnels host a mesmerising array of eateries, where you can sample omiyage (regional food souvenirs, *see* p. 8), and standing bars for a craft beer or sake (*see* p. 11). Then there is the shopping … Hankyu Department Store (*see* p. 5) is a multi-floor complex with a truly memorable frontage (and atmospheric Christmas windows if you are there in December).

Once you are above ground things don't get any less chaotic – or any less inspirational. From the looming tower and sprawling views of the Umeda Sky Building (*see* p. 2) and a plethora of vast shopping malls, neon jungles, old-world enclaves and hidden alleys – Shin Umeda Shokudo Street (*see* p. 7) to behemoths like Yodobashi (*see* p. 5) – exploring the station environs will never be dull. And if you want to try the city's famed delicacy fugu (pufferfish), head to Kitashinchi (*see* p. 12). Train nerds will be in heaven at Hankyu Osaka–Umeda station and Hanshin–Umeda station, where you will be transported to Cute Japanese Train Land (we made that place up but it fits the bill!).

→ *Osaka station, Tempozan Ferris Wheel, temperature sign*

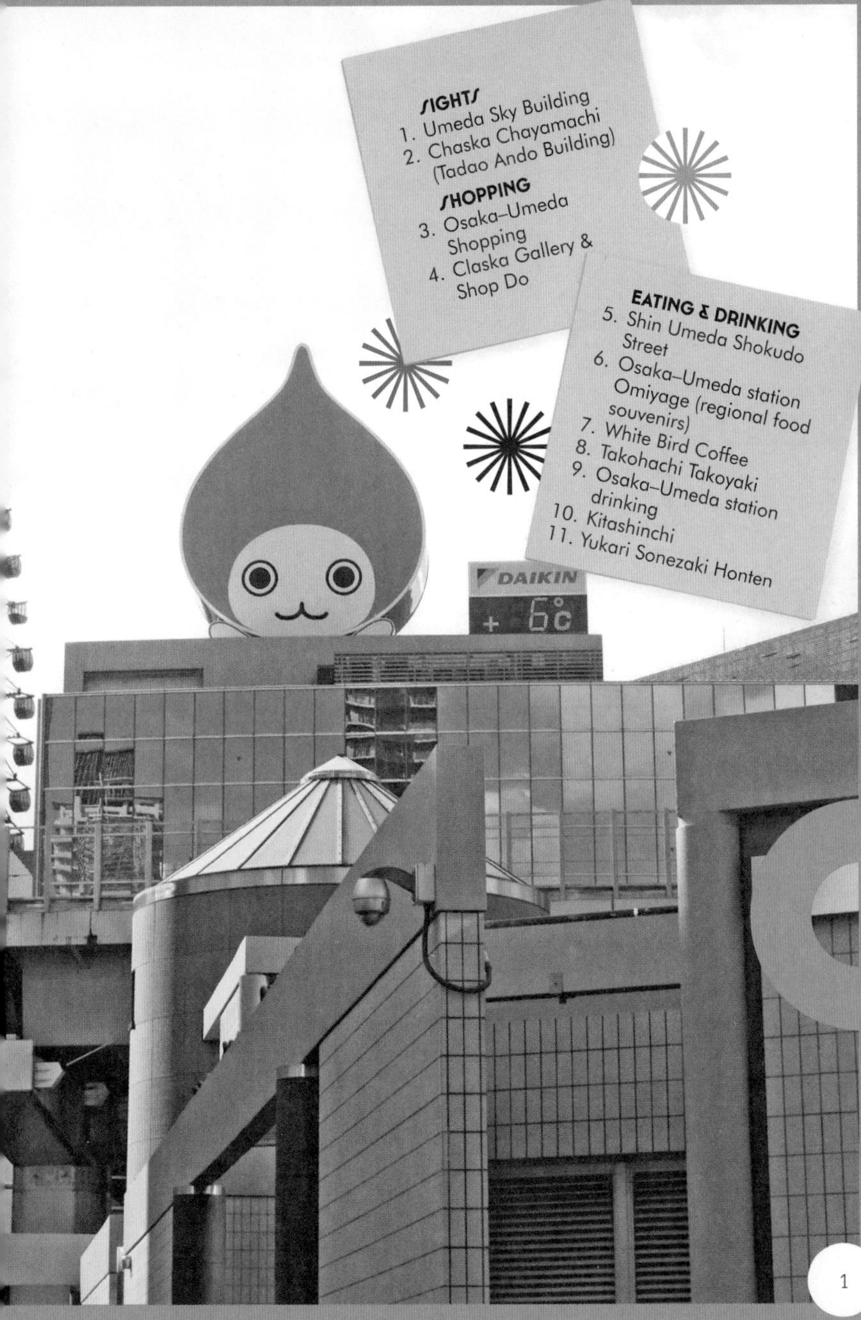

SIGHTS

1. Umeda Sky Building
2. Chaska Chayamachi (Tadao Ando Building)

SHOPPING

3. Osaka–Umeda Shopping
4. Claska Gallery & Shop Do

EATING & DRINKING

5. Shin Umeda Shokudo Street
6. Osaka–Umeda station Omiyage (regional food souvenirs)
7. White Bird Coffee
8. Takohachi Takoyaki
9. Osaka–Umeda station drinking
10. Kitashinchi
11. Yukari Sonezaki Honten

1 UMEDA SKY BUILDING

1-1-88 Oyodonaka, Kita-ku
6440 3899
Mon–Sun 9.30am–10.30pm
Osaka station, exit 4
[MAP p. 164 C1]

If you want to see a feat of remarkable Japanese engineering, then this is it: two towering pillars of glass and steel connected by two floating escalators and a roof with a huge porthole, designed by master of scale Hiroshi Hara. The vast porthole in the centre of the building is one of the main attractions, but you can't miss riding the 'invisible' escalators up to the **Floating Garden Observatory**, a verdant 39th floor open-air deck with dazzling views. We like to head up at sunset, when everything lights up on both the deck and below, making it even more spectacular. The words 'dizzy heights' have never been more apt and if you suffer from vertigo this experience probably isn't for you, so head instead to the basement of the building, which features **Takimikoji**, a faithful reconstruction of a traditional Showa-era shopping street. There are Osaka specialty food restaurants and even the toilets are designed with elements of a Showa-era bathhouse.

POCKET TIP

Surrounding Shin Umeda City has many landscaped gardens with blossoms in springtime and fireflies at night. Tadao Ando's sculpture, *Wall of Hope*, can be found at the end of the New Satoyama landscaped garden.

2 CHASKA CHAYAMACHI (TADAO ANDO BUILDING)

Harmonie Embrassee, Rokko Island Office, The Antante, 4th floor 5-15 Koyocho, Higashi, Nanda-ku
6376 2255
Mon–Sun 10am–6pm
Osaka–Umeda station, exit H8
[MAP p. 166 A3]

An Osaka native who started small and became legendary, Tadao Ando's ultimate 'return home' statement is this stunning building: a triangular sliver of office-space-meets-residence, set amongst a part of town populated by faceless blocks and elevated freeways. The top layer of the building is a platform holding a latticed 'thin slice of cake' shaped structure, which is home to a boutique hotel, reception space and chapel. Ando didn't do the interior – his minimalist aesthetic is forsaken for semi-luxe rooms that you can only visit if you are 'Just Married'. If you're an architecture buff, you'll appreciate the perfect meditation on commerce versus aesthetic. In the end it's the exterior that wins, the metal wedge slices defiantly through the skyline like an axe head.

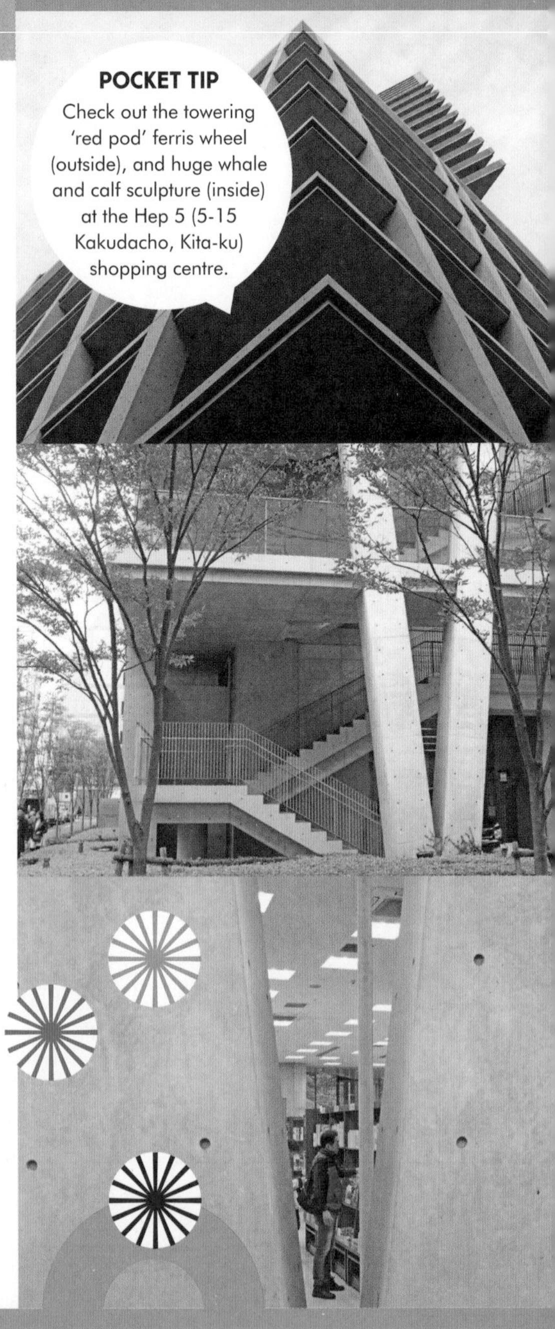

POCKET TIP

Check out the towering 'red pod' ferris wheel (outside), and huge whale and calf sculpture (inside) at the Hep 5 (5-15 Kakudacho, Kita-ku) shopping centre.

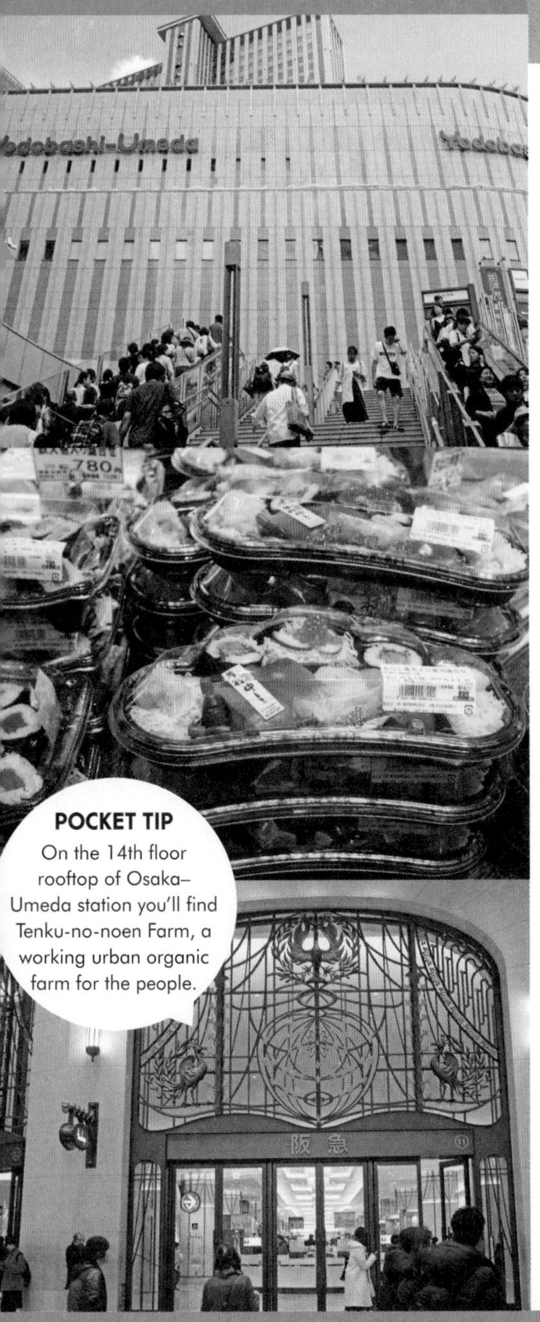

POCKET TIP

On the 14th floor rooftop of Osaka–Umeda station you'll find Tenku-no-noen Farm, a working urban organic farm for the people.

3 OSAKA–UMEDA SHOPPING

Kita-ku

The Osaka–Umeda station area must have a more diverse range of shops, eateries and malls than anywhere else in the world. Most of them are connected by a staggering array of tunnels and byways (we always get lost in them) that connect with the main department stores and rail stations. At the **Hankyu Department Store**'s flagship building (8-7 Kakudacho), you can shop luxe Japanese and international brands, but don't miss the must-see entryway of intricate and decorative iron-work from the Taisho-era (Japan's Art Deco-period, 1912–26). The standout food market on the basement floors is a great place to grab some of the food souvenirs that Osaka is famous for (*see* p. 8). Pop up to the station's exit 4 to find **Yodobashi**'s (1-1 Ofukacho) impressive curved building, housing tech and electronic goods over seven floors. Some of Japan's best department stores: **Loft** (16-7 Chayamachi), **Kiddy Land** (Hankyu Sanbangai North Building 1-1-3 Shibata) and music mecca **Disk Union** (1F ACTIII 15-17 Doyamacho), are all within an easy walk of station exits.

4 CLASKA GALLERY & SHOP DO

7th floor Hanshin Umeda Corner 1-13-13, Umeda, Kita-ku
6450 8960
Mon–Sun 10am–8pm
Osaka–Umeda station
[MAP p. 165 B2]

If you're shopping for immaculately curated homewares and simple, but elegant, fashion that won't poke fun at your budget, Claska is your Osaka lifestyle store. Its contemporary style is both at odds with rough-edged Osaka and the perfect fit for a city that needs a little flair and attitude in the everyday. The Claska shop **Do** has a range of designer products with a traditional Japanese spin, giving them a timeless quality. Shop for glassware and cutlery, as well as themed homewares and playful ceramics. The women's clothing is functional but effortlessly chic and this also extends to the range of jewellery, textiles and furniture. Contemporary but with a distinct nod to the past, Claska celebrates artisan creation and attention to detail, and spins it for the discerning customer, giving you unique take-home keepsakes.

5 SHIN UMEDA SHOKUDO STREET

9-26 Kakuda, Kita-ku
6312 1869
Hours vary
Osaka–Umeda station, Midousuji exit
[MAP p. 165 B1]

In this atmospheric sanctum of old Osaka, you'll find many longstanding restaurants that specialise in shokudo (simple home-style lunch and dinner sets) hidden away in the tunnels under Osaka–Umeda station. Created around 1950 with 18 shops, Shokudo Street originally attracted already established businesses from around the area. Now almost 100 shops snake around the small burrows and rabbit warrens in the belly of the station – most with the charmingly retro original signage. We find Shokudo Street a perfect spot to experience hashigo (bar hopping), where you can flit from bar to bar trying the drinks and the tapas-style food. There are a range of eateries in the atmospheric corridors, from quality okonomiyaki (savoury omelette), to kushikatsu (fried meats or vegetables on skewers), yakitori, oden and udon (and the occasional French wine bar). Osaka is known for kui-daore (eat 'til you drop) and you can certainly do that here – without breaking the bank.

6 OSAKA-UMEDA STATION OMIYAGE (REGIONAL FOOD SOUVENIRS)

When it comes to food, Osaka has a reputation to uphold and, here, in the small stores and mini-marts in the station corridors and hubs, you'll find the city's frankly mind-boggling range of food souvenirs. Our favourites include roll cake, crème caramel pudding – check out **Pom Pom Purin** pudding cafe (Basement 2F 1-1-3 Shibata, Kita-ku) for a cute interior with character-themed everything – as well as takoyaki flavoured 'Jagabee' calbee fries, Osaka banana (like Tokyo banana but with added chocolate) and apple cake. You'll also find Osaka's popular **551 Horai** (multiple stores), a chain selling shumai buns and dumplings to go. Other must-have take-aways include **Kuidaore Taro Pudding** (multiple stores) and **Uncle Rikuro Cheese Cake** (Basement 1F Daimaru 3-1-1). Pick up a tako (octopus) keyring, soft toy or other souvenir – the tako is one of Osaka's symbols!

POCKET TIP

Outside, to Osaka-Umeda station's east, the approach to Tsuyu no Tenjinsha shrine is a colourful alley crammed with omiyage stores and eateries.

7 WHITE BIRD COFFEE

1st floor National Hwy Bldg,
2-1-12 Sonezaki, Kita-ku
6809 3769
Mon–Sat 11am–10.30pm, Sun 11am–10pm
Higashi Umeda station, exit 4
[MAP p. 165 C3]

A short walk from Osaka–Umeda station, through rowdy streets and past towering skyscrapers, on a corner by the side of an overpass on a major intersection, you'll find the welcoming front doors of White Bird Coffee. Once you are inside, the outside world melts away in a wash of cool jazz. The style here is bowl cuts, stripes and berets. Come for the coffee, made to perfection with single-origin beans, and iced-coffee served in a jar. Stay for the ambience – wooden tables, wicker baskets, subway tiles, low lighting and mismatched furniture. Desserts are over the top, so you have to try them, including (depending on the season) strawberry milk, delicious coffee jelly, served in a tall glass with lashings of cream on top, and chestnut pound cake. There's a good range of alcoholic drinks so if you are wanting to kick back with a drink while listening to jazz and looking out onto a major sky-high freeway, then White Bird is the nest you've been looking for.

8 TAKOHACHI TAKOYAKI

Osaka–Umeda station,
North Mall, Whity Bldg, 2-4-6
Komatsubaracho, Kita-ku
Mon–Sun 10am–9pm
[MAP p. 165 B2]

If you are in the mood for super-fresh takoyaki (octopus dumplings), Takohachi do an interesting spin on the Osakan street-food staple. It is one of a plethora of on-the-go eateries and standing bars in the Whity Building, but it features an open kitchen, where the chef makes the dumplings right in front of you. It only has 10–12 seats and the fast-moving crowd is mostly solo travellers and day shoppers ordering lunch sets with the signature fluffy dumplings and Takohachi's unique accompaniment: a light dashi broth and generous side serves of okonomiyaki (savoury omelette) or squid ink yakisoba (stir-fried noodles). The great-value sets also include booze or a cold drink. The food arrives 'without makeup', allowing you to apply your own mayonnaise and barbecue sauce, and the patterns you make say more about your personality than a psychiatry test (just try to master the perfect Okonomiyaki criss-cross or web design).

9 OSAKA–UMEDA STATION DRINKING

Craft beer is a big deal in many cities and Osaka mixes it up with the best of them. **Craft Beer Base** (Osaka–station First Building 1-3-1, Umeda, Kita-ku) is rowdy and fun with four craft beers on tap. **Craft Beer House Molto!!** (31F Hankyu Grand Building 8-47 Kakudacho, Kita-ku) has high-level drinking (and by high-level we mean the 31st floor of the Hankyu Grand Building). **Craft Beer Market** (3-1-3 Umeda, Kita-ku) is a popular Tokyo craft beer haunt making its foray into Osaka. If you prefer sake, try **Asano Nihonshuten Umeda**, (2-17 Taiyujicho Kita-ku), a breezy modern standing bar with over 150 brands of sake, mostly made in and around Osaka. **Shimada Shoten** (3-5-1 Itachibori, Nishi-ku) is a classic sake bar that dates back to 1954; we love the little nook with cosy furniture, warm woods and a small library. The space promotes a hushed reverence for sake, and the owner even prefers all conversations to be about sake!

10 KITASHINCHI

Kita-ku
[MAP p. 165 A4]

To the south of Osaka–Umeda station you'll find an old business and Geisha district – now one of Osaka's most popular entertainment hubs. Here there's a plethora of nightclubs, bars and eateries frolicking in a neon playground. There is plenty to grab your attention, with karaoke, seedy dives, oddball-themed cafes, shifty alleyways and all-night party live houses. More importantly however, the area specialises in one of Osaka's symbols: fugu (puffer-fish). If you want to visit a quality fugu restaurant to try one of Japan's legendary delicacies, this is the place to do it. Head to one of the following: **Fugu Tenjin** (1-7-13 Sonezaki), **Yumefuku** (2-2-1 Sonezaki), **Yakifugu Yumeteppo Kitashinchi** (1-4-7 Dojima), **Yakifugu Yafuku** (1-3-33 Dojima) or **Fuguyoshi Kitashinchi** (1-3-8 Sonezaki).

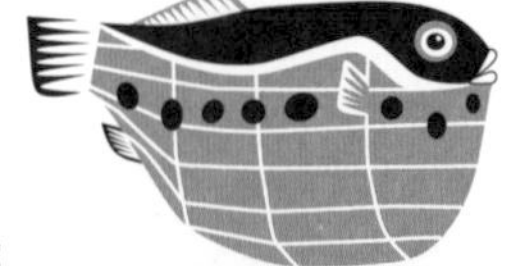

POCKET TIP

Visit nearby Tsuyu no Tenjinsha (Ohatsu Tenjin) shrine, the setting for the tragic and romantic bunraku puppet play, The Love Suicides of Sonezaki (2 Chome-5-4 Sonezaki, Kita-ku).

11 YUKARI SONEZAKI HONTEN

2-14-13 Sonezaki, Kita-ku
Mon–Sun 11am–1am
[MAP p. 165 B2]

Make your way down colourful Ohatsutenjin-dori arcade and look for the large red sign, red lantern, photographic menu and the queue. You'll know that you've arrived at popular okonomiyaki (savoury omelette) joint Yukari Sonezaki Honten, feeding hungry Osakans since 1950. It hasn't changed much since then, with its mustard-coloured furniture, wallpaper and a soundtrack of swing, big-band jazz and happy customers. Order up an apple sparkling wine highball or two. Okonomiyaki here is theatre: cooked at your table on a hot-plate and ingredients are piled high. It takes 15–20 minutes until it's perfectly browned, during which time the staff magically appear and shuffle or flip the okonomiyaki. Yukari have their own special mayonnaise and barbecue sauce, so add it liberally. The menu features a broad choice, including a Korean-style kimchi or yakitori filling and hungry punters can choose to supersize (so very Osaka). Pescatarians have plenty of seafood options and vegetarians can try the cheese and rice cake special or one of a variety of sides.

NAKAZAKICHO

Unpretentious, un-signposted and cool, yet just a stone's throw away from the frenzied pace of Osaka–Umeda station, Nakazakicho is a random pocket of indie bars, cute pop-up shops and hole-in-the-wall eateries. The precinct is made up of small and windy streets, it's great for people-watching, chatting over coffee and vintage shopping. A lot of the youthful vigour here spirals out from the Senriyama campus of Kansai University and its impressive attached bookstore, Tsutaya Bookstore MeRise (*see* p. 22).

Some of Osaka's best coffee can be found in Nakazakicho, like Haiku Coffee Roasters (*see* p. 19) and The Gut's Coffee (*see* p. 19). Vintage is almost as prevalent here as it is in Amerikamura (*see* p. 74) and can be found in a range of standout stores, including Green Pepe (*see* p. 16) and Elulu by Jam (*see* p. 16). Whether it's zakka (miscellaneous things, *see* p.18), retro toys, pre-loved clothing, quirky jewellery or rustic, secretive cafes in hidden alleys, you'll find plenty of options. Small businesses here have a natural retro charm, set up in old houses with repurposed furniture from nearby antique emporiums. Salon de AManTo (*see* p. 20) is the creative heart of the area, two inspiring spaces set up by an art collective. Public Kitchen (*see* p. 21), perfects a take on teishoku, the Japanese rustic, organic small-plate meal-set. Inventive, reactionary, cute and cool, Nakazakicho is unmissable indie Osaka.

→ *Green Pepe vintage store*

SHOPPING

1. Vintage stores
2. Zakka stores

EATING & DRINKING

3. Coffee
4. Salon de AManTo
5. Public Kitchen
6. Picco Latte
7. Noon + Cafe

1 VINTAGE STORES

Kita-ku

Nakazakicho's treasure-trove of thrift stores have us flipping through racks of pre-loved merchandise for hours. For vintage with a dose of super-cute, head to **Elulu by Jam** (2-4-31, Nakazakinishi). Snap some pics of the pink brick frontage and fluoro Marilyn Monroe sign before shopping the range. **Pigsty Vintage** (3-3-10, Nakazakinishi) has a constantly evolving selection, which they 'workshop', so you can mix and match pieces to create a new look. **Green Pepe** (3-1-12, Nakazaki) has '60s and '70s paraphernalia and toys arranged in a haphazard space. Take your inner kid to **Two Elephants** (1-11-2, Nakazakinishi) for stuffed shelves of vintage toys. **Spia** (1-6-21, Nakazakinishi) has a charming cafe upstairs and well curated vintage clothing downstairs. **Haraiso** (4-3-45, Nakazakinishi) is a vintage store and cafe housed in a beautiful building. The orange box surrounded by corrugated iron is **Used Clothing Shop Orange** (1-8-28, Nakazakinishi). Be sure to search the streets, this is just the tip of the thrift-berg.

STAR WARS
PINOCCHIO

2 ZAKKA STORES

Kita-ku

Around the streets of crafty and creative Nakazakicho, you'll find many small craft and zakka (miscellaneous things) stores. There are some 130 stores that have popped up in renovated townhouses, wedged between office blocks and in alleys and lanes. It makes for an enjoyable wander, discovering places for yourself, but here are some of our favourites. **Jam Pot** (3-2-31, Nakazaki) is a tiny space dedicated to small handmade jewellery, homewares and accessories made by Japanese artists and crafters. Sibling store **Guignol** (2-3-28, Nakazaki) delves into the realm of creepy cute with French gothic and Victorian steampunk-themed curiosities, including sinister dolls, ghoulish jewellery, tarot cards and astrology charts. **Only Planet** (3-1-6, Nakazaki) is a menagerie of tiny crafted animals and animal-themed gifts with an ecological slant. **Ma-Jo** (4-2-12, Nakazakinishi) is a cafe that also sells cat craft. **Lolotte Candle** (1-7-11, Nakazakinishi) sells cute handmade animal candles. If you're a fan of cute homewares, handmade goods and cafes with more charm and less space, you'll be in heaven in Nakazakicho.

POCKET TIP

If you haven't had enough cute, head to Simako (1-7-35, Nakazakinishi, Kita-ku) for an adorable cake or Café Arabiq (3-2-14, Nakazaki, Kita-ku), which is full of creepy dolls and sells coffee with sugar candy topping.

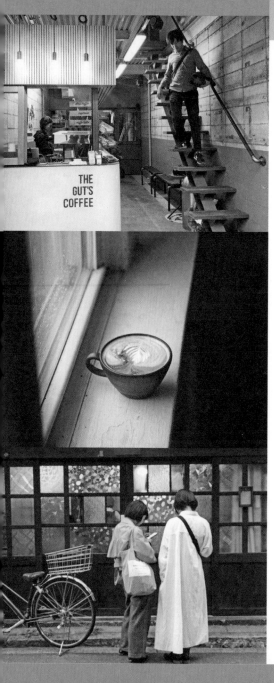

3 COFFEE

Kita-ku

Shopping in Nakazakicho requires energy, so luckily this little hood makes some of the best quality contemporary brews in the city to give you the pick-me-up you'll need. **Haiku Coffee Roasters** (3-23-3, Kurosakicho) is one of our favourite hangouts, they do a premium pour-over coffee and pair it with their cake of the day. **The Gut's Coffee** (3-2-29, Nakazaki) is set up in a sleek, yet rustic garage-style, space beneath their signage and design firm. Try their delicious drip coffee and pick up an iced-tea or lemonade on a hot day. **Utena Kissaten** cafe (1-8-23, Nakazakinishi) is housed in another amazing vintage building, complete with an interior of warm dark wood and retro furniture. Come for the coffee, stay for the cinnamon or jam toast and cheesecake. At **89 Café** (3-9-1, Nakazakinishi), you can get a cup of the naughty bean and then hire a kimono for a stylish stroll around town.

4 SALON DE AMANTO

1-7-26 Nakazakinishi, Kita-ku
6371 5840
Mon–Sun 12pm–10pm
Nakazakicho station, exit 1
[MAP p. 167 E2]

Housed in an old printing factory, AManTo is run by a collective of local artists as an event space, cafe and bar with unfussy, inexpensive meals. The first thing you'll notice is the gorgeous overgrown exterior: you can hardly get inside because the hedge is so thick. Inside, furniture, low lights, crammed bookshelves and trimmings are recycled and repurposed, making an atmosphere conducive to creative discussions. Simple lunches like curry (a steal at around ¥500) extend to 3pm, as do cakes that complement your coffee. The bar kicks in later, so you can continue your intellectual conversations into the night. Various events come in the form of movie screenings, theatre, dance and intimate music performances, which often occur at random, giving you added entertainment while you eat lunch or relax with a drink. As an added bonus, profits are donated to an organisation that feeds children in need.

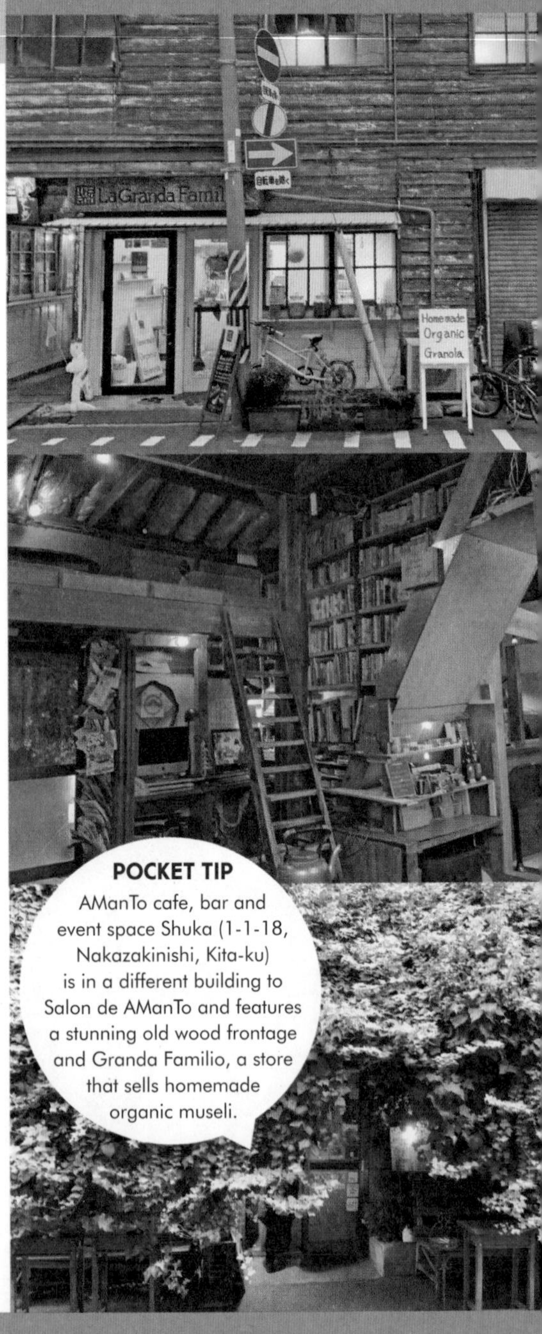

POCKET TIP

AManTo cafe, bar and event space Shuka (1-1-18, Nakazakinishi, Kita-ku) is in a different building to Salon de AManTo and features a stunning old wood frontage and Granda Familio, a store that sells homemade organic museli.

5 PUBLIC KITCHEN

1-9-12 Nakazakinishi, Kita-ku
6375 7339
Fri–Sun 11.30am–9pm, Tues–Thurs 11.30am–9.30pm
Nakazakicho station, exit 1
[MAP p. 167 D2]

If you've been hitting the booze or snaffling too much of the wonderful but less-than-healthy street foods that Osaka has to offer, head to Public Kitchen for a spiritual cleanse. Slip down the narrow lane and emerge before the cafe's sliding door. The food reflects the space: simple, rustic and organic. The cafe operates a farm in Hyogo prefecture and the food is sourced from there, so it's a real farm-to-table experience. Both lunch and dinner are served teishoku-style, a set meal where you will usually get a soup, rice, a main and a side dish all served together. Choose from croquettes, fried chicken and a wide range of healthy salads and vegetables. It tastes good and it's good for you.

POCKET TIP

After a day of shopping, power on with some live music at relaxed bar Kandylion (3-5-14 Nakazaki Kita-ku) or power down with a soak at Hamura Hot Spring Bath (1-7-18 Nakazakinichi Kita-ku).

6 PICCO LATTE

4-1-8 Nakazakinishi, Kita-ku
6467 8695
Mon–Sun 11.30am–7pm
Nakazakicho station, exit 1
[MAP p. 167 D2]

The sign says Dry Flower and Cafe and that sums up what must be one of the most unique concepts in cafe culture. Picco Latte dry their own flowers and use them to decorate and enhance the flavour of a range of some of the most decorative drinks and food you've ever seen. Coffee, smoothies, parfait desserts and cheesecake pops are transformed into photo-worthy vignettes, laced with vibrant flowers. The visual spectacle ensures constant crowds are lined up at the front door (so much so that a time limit of one hour has been introduced). The cheesecake pops are topped with fresh fruit and flowers, and are as stunning as the dried flower-strewn ceiling. Don't forget to take away their picturesque bottles of strawberry, mango, black honey or matcha milk.

POCKET TIP

Tsutaya Bookstore MeRise (1-5 Tsurunocho, Kita-ku) is a contemporary bookstore with crammed bookshelves from floor to ceiling, with a great cafe and plenty of study spaces.

7 NOON + CAFE

3-3-8 Nakazakinishi, Kita-ku
6373 4919
Mon–Sun 11am–11pm
Nakazakicho station, exit 3
[MAP p. 166 B3]

Noon is a cosy daytime cafe and bar, with towering ceilings, hanging lights, peeling walls and exposed pipes. You can get a premium pour-over or an affogato and, if you're hungry, they serve hot dogs, burgers and bagels, and continue the American food theme with New York cheesecake. Noon also runs one of Nakazakicho's late-night clubs. Draconian and outdated local laws have threatened the club's operation, giving it the feel of a speakeasy (the fact that you can smoke inside adds to that feeling of an illicit hideaway) as they battle the powers that be. Things seem to be swinging their way however and, for the moment, you can catch indie music nights, like Deeperama with DJ Sprinkles Mitsuki, and British Pavillion with DJ Groover. Make sure to catch an exhibition at upstairs gallery **Oops! Here I Go Again**. Note: Noon + Cafe is cash only.

FUKUSHIMA & HIGOBASHI

Within easy walking distance of Osaka–Umeda station (*see* p. xii) lies a pocket of unusual architecture, tiny craft stores, inventive locals, and young upstarts opening cafes, galleries, vintage stores and eateries. It's the face of new creative Osaka, and more crucially, one that hasn't hit the mainstream psyche just yet. The oddball futuristic modernism of the Gate Tower Building (*see* p. 26) and Kisho Kurokawa's International Convention Center (*see* p. 27) mark the area out as an architectural pilgrimage. It's the way a city could have looked in the 1960s and beyond, but that all fell by the wayside in the face of rapid modernism.

Both Fukushima and Higobashi have stations with tiny backstreets, and lanes filled with izakayas (pubs with small-plate food) and bars, with cafes a distinct international flavour, and a leaning towards Italian, French and Indian cuisine. Takamura Wine and Coffee Roasters (*see* p. 34) brings sophistication (and a whole lot of wine) to Fukushima's backstreets and Graf (*see* p. 30) adds to that with a keenly nuanced collection of designer homewares. So, take a walk and explore this burgeoning new precinct to discover a side of Osaka far away from the ebb and overflow of the city centre.

→ *Eatery near Shin Fukushima station*

SIGHTS

1. Gate Tower Building
2. Osaka International Convention Center

SHOPPING

3. Essential Store
4. Shibakawa Building

SHOPPING & EATING

5. Graf

EATING & DRINKING

6. Local Osaka
7. Takamura Wine and Coffee Roasters

1 GATE TOWER BUILDING

5-4-21 Fukushima,
Fukushima-ku
Osaka–Umeda station, exit 6-2
[MAP p. 164 C3]

The Japanese are problem solvers so it follows that if a building is in the way of a road, they would just make the road go through the building. This is exactly what architect Nishihara Kenchiku Sekkei Jimusho did with the Gate Tower Building, an accommodating skyscraper that redefines what a city can look like in the face of growing urbanisation. Often referred to as The Beehive, cars swarm through the fifth to seventh floors of the building from the Umeda off-ramp. It's classic Osaka and puts a smile on your face and makes you think about the limitations of other cityscapes. It's a regular feature on the worldwide lists of jaw-dropping urban development. A bonus is that the best view and photographable shots of the building are from the Umeda Sky Building (*see* p. 2), pairing together two spectacular Osaka new builds.

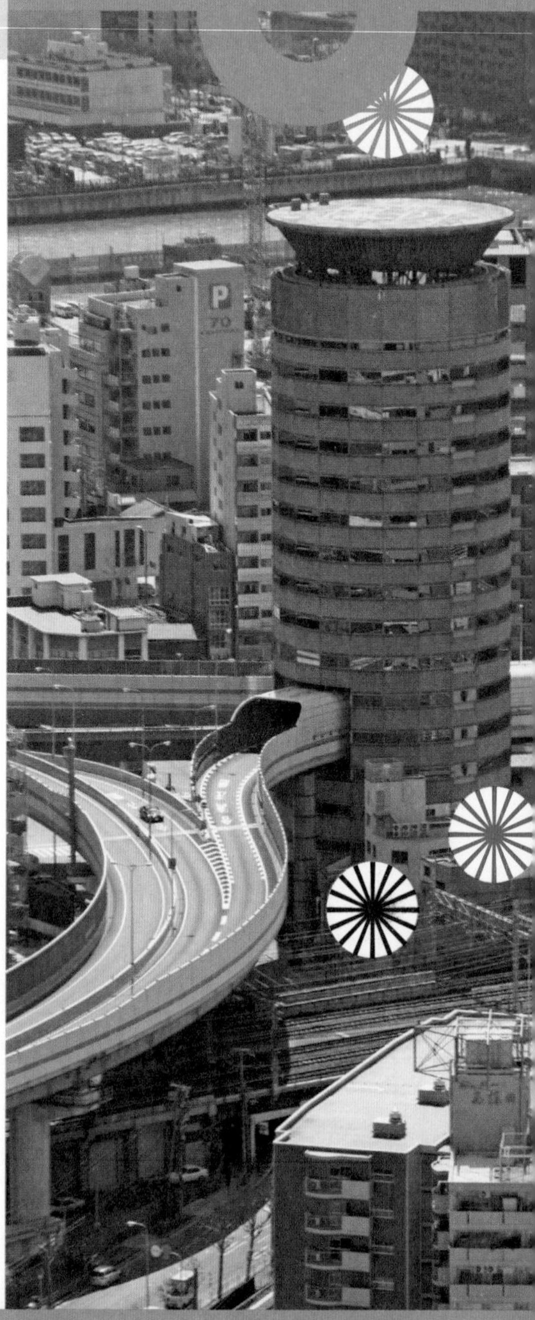

POCKET TIP

The National Museum of Art Osaka (4-2-55 Nakonoshima, Kita-ku) is an underground gallery showcasing European modern art and post-war contemporary art – the above ground 'steel bamboo plumage' design is spectacular.

2 OSAKA INTERNATIONAL CONVENTION CENTER

5-3-51 Nakanoshima, Kita-ku
Mon–Sun 9am–9pm
Nakanoshima station, exit 2
[MAP p. 162 A2]

Also known as the 'Grand Cube', this building is a youthful block of steel from 1996, a towering square of metal with a conical flourish for a crown and an urban garden growing in its central arch. Kisho Kurakawa was the creator of two of Tokyo's most memorable buildings: the Nakagin Capsule Tower and the National Art Center, and he certainly stamps his mark on Osaka here. It's a rare chance for architecture fans to get a glimpse of an actual Metabolism building – a movement dreamed up by post-war architectural Futurists, whose designs rarely got past the planning stage. A kind of soft Brutalism, it takes into account the needs of the people, while addressing the constraints of the immediate environment. Inside, it's crammed with cafes, restaurants, grand halls and hotels. A kind of mini biosphere set among the open streets, an artwork, a haven and a functional building all in one, it encapsulates the essence of the Metabolism movement.

3 ESSENTIAL STORE

2-2-18 Edobori, Nishi-ku
6443 3519
Thurs–Tues 11am–7.30pm
Higobashi station, exit 9
[MAP p. 164 A4]

A chic, plain white building in a corner of Higobashi hides a cabinet of curiosities. The interior of this shop looks like a museum of natural history. Step through the portal into a world of enchantment, where soaring ceilings with wooden beams dangle ferns and mismatched lights into the open space, while greenery sprouts from corners and walls, and statues and chandeliers fight for floor space with a range of trinkets and oddments. The title seems ironic, as what they sell here seems anything but essential. Shop the range to find that special something that will add a whimsical note to your home decor. Locally handmade brooches and glassware co-habit shelves with eccentric objet d'art and homewares with a hint of humour. Lamps with attitude, second-hand vinyl and out-of-place furniture all add up to an archaeological dig of bric-a-brac and accoutrements that you never thought you needed until now.

4 SHIBAKAWA BUILDING

3-3-3 Fushimimachi, Chuo-ku
Hours vary
Yoyodabashi station, exit 11
[MAP p. 163 F3]

The Shibakawa Building is a bohemian enclave brimming with character. It's an eclectic mish-mash of styles, a true original, with echoes of early 20th-century Europe, a curved stone facade, columns and elements of South American Inca design and topped with a Spanish tiled roof. It was built in 1927 by Shibakawa Matashiro and once home to a Bride School, where women learnt how to excel in cooking, cleaning and managing the budget. The space has now been repurposed into a shopping and eating hub over four floors. The cosy and eclectic **Mole and Hosoi Coffees** on the ground floor is one of our favourite hangouts. It's like an old-fashioned kissaten (coffee house), with personal service, a bar and gallery. Don't miss **Scene**, also on the ground floor, for sharp, yet casual, clothing and footwear. Pop into **Ricordo** on the second floor for exquisite designer glassware, before heading to the third floor to **Yumiko Iihoshi's** beautiful porcelain and ceramics store.

5 GRAF

4-1-9 Nakanoshima, Kita-ku
Tues–Sun 11am–7pm
Nakanoshima station, exit 3
[MAP p. 162 B2]

Run by Decorative Mode Number 3, a collective of six creatives and craftspeople, Graf is the face of 21st-century design in Osaka: a homewares store, gallery and eatery with a dynamic mix of high style without pretense. The building is stunning, yet simple and signals the store's intent – that the everyday can be enhanced by beautiful design. Inside, the group's work is showcased among the Graf Collection. Furniture is complemented by a range of homewares intended to convey the designers' 'feeling' to the user – like their fun food-themed tableware or simple-yet-stylish hanging lights. Specialised craft from the surrounding area adds local colour to the already impressive selection. The group's design aesthetic extends to the food in the second-floor restaurant – one of the team is a chef. After shopping, you can hit the downstairs cafe for some well-designed coffee and cake. Graf embodies Fukushima's reputation as the up-and-coming coffee, wine and food hub of Osaka.

6 LOCAL OSAKA

Underneath the train tracks, in quiet pockets and down the thin alleyways between Fukushima and Shin Fukushima stations, you'll find small bars and cafes, a real taste of local Osaka. Walk from Shin Fukushima towards the Osaka International Convention Center (*see* p. 27) and you'll find plenty of Japanese, Italian, Spanish and French eateries. Our pick is **Sumibiyaki Unagi No Nedoko** (2-6-11 Higashishinsaibashi Chuo-ku), a popular local eel restaurant, and **Salmonbal Partia** (8-1-43 Fukushima, Fukushima-ku) is where we head for Italian. For burgers and beer, we like **Kannosuke** (3 Chome-8-10 Fukushima, Fukushima-ku) or, for fresh seafood and international wines, try **Spiny Oyster Bar** (3 Chome-7-24 Fukushima, Fukushima-ku). **Pit Master Vamos BBQ** (8-1-1 Fukushima, Fukushima-ku) does rowdy Mexican. We love the kakigori (shaved ice) at **Cafe 12** (2-3-12 Fukushima, Fukushima-ku), although cheesecake is their specialty.

日本酒と
親の言う
ことは、後から
効いてくる
忘年会

もつ鍋
おでん
串かつ
お持ち帰り 出来ます!!
New スタッフ大募集!!
バニラ
マンゴー

7 TAKAMURA WINE AND COFFEE ROASTERS

2-2-18 Edobori, Nishi-ku
6443 3519
Thurs–Tues 11am–7.30pm
Higobashi station, exit 9
[MAP p. 162 B3]

One of the leading lights in the new wave of Osaka coffee is this concept store done Osaka-style, with a cafe, eatery, winery and shopping space. Its objective is simple: make great wine and coffee available to all at an affordable price point. The interior's impressive central 'birdcage' sits in a modernist and minimalist space, a great contrast to Osaka's messy and relaxed style. The range of wines is staggering: over two thousand choices from various parts of the globe. You can taste or drink on the premises or shop from the well-stocked shelves. A new breed of talented baristas also puts the coffee front and centre – the coffee culture matches the wine culture, with varieties, blends, flavour notes and brewing techniques, all manifested in excellent pour-over coffee. Huge roasting machines make the space look like a coffee museum. The coffee and wine worlds are at your fingertips here, so stroll the aisles dropping bottles and bags of beans into your cart.

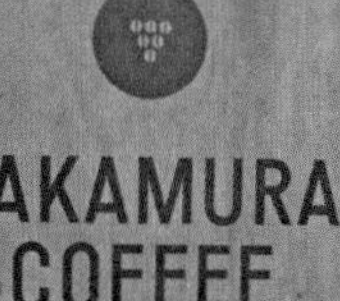

POCKET TIP

A pop-up Takamura can be found in the impressive Hanshin Department Store in Osaka–Umeda station.

NIPPONBASHI & DEN DEN TOWN

South-east of Osaka–Namba station you'll find tech-obsessed Nipponbashi, featuring Osaka's main electronics area and Otaku (geek nerd) district. Den Den Town (*see* p. 38) and Ota Road (*see* p. 39) have a myriad of stores selling electronics, gadgets and up-to-the-minute tech, including all of Japan's famous gadget brands. Placate your inner uber-nerd and shop the figurine, trading cards and computer game merchandise stores or drop some coins into a gashapon vending machine. It's great for kids, large or small. And if you're feeling nostalgic for retro toys or are desperate to fill that gap in your manga character collection, head to Hero Gangu (*see* p. 40).

In stark contrast, nearby Kuromon Ichiba Market (*see* p. 41) is a lively seafood mecca, full of vociferous hawkers, hole-in-the-wall eateries and friendly stalls selling a colourful (and sometimes alarming) array of whatever's been liberated from the ocean that morning. It's perfect for an early morning seafood rice bowl or a coffee in one of the old-school coffee houses. Street food opportunities can be found in and around Nipponbashi, including at Naruto Taiyaki Hompo (*see* p. 43) selling one of Japan's fast-food dessert staples: sweet fish-shaped pastries.

→ *Otaku-themed Lawson convenience store*

SHOPPING
1. Den Den Town
2. Ota Road
3. Hero Gangu
SHOPPING & EATING
4. Kuromon Ichiba Market
EATING
5. Ibuki Coffee Kuromon
6. Naruto Taiyaki Hompo
土地家屋調査士
LAWSON STATION
DRAGON QUEST XI S
大阪
POL

1 DEN DEN TOWN

[MAP p. 173 E4]

You can easily get lost in the maze-like electronics mecca of Den Den Town (also known as Denki machi – electric town), a couple of blocks dedicated to all things electrical. The many stores are devoted to anything that needs a power source in order to work: appliances, new tech, robots, devices and distractions. Here you will drool over cinema screen-size TVs, countless brands of rice-cookers, the latest almost-sentient vacuuming robot or a smart phone that's smarter than the last one you bought. Floors and floors of gadgetry await your perusal, while down below in lanes and arcades, smaller stores have their own particular specialties and compete with the nearby megaliths by using deep knowledge and attentive service. They are also happy to negotiate on prices – something that is mostly considered rude in Japan. It's definitely worth shopping around for the best deal. Once a major hub for second-hand homewares, books and clothing, the area still has many small vintage stores squeezed between the electronics outlets. Opening times vary but most stores run until 9pm.

2 OTA ROAD

Stores usually open 11am–9pm [MAP p. 173 E3]

With the major electronic players siphoning customers away from the smaller electronic stores, a shift has taken place around Den Den Town (*see* p. 38) and its enclaves. Smaller stores have instead started catering to collectors, anime watchers, cosplayers, sci-fi obsessives, model makers and vintage gamers – otaku as they are known in Japan. Ota (Otaku) Road is set up as a one-stop shopping strip for fan boys and fan girls. **Pokémon**, **One Piece**, **Gundam** robots – Ota Road caters to them all in a variety of stores. Specialist shops with in-the-know staff are everywhere to help you with your manga madness or cosplay compulsion. As you would expect, the area is colourful, loud and populated by people in character outfits, maid cafe spruikers, the pop and ping of video games and the potential for a frightening bill when you succumb to the allure of that vintage character collectible. Dweeb megastores like **Animate** hold regular events, meet and greets, and dress-up days.

3 HERO GANGU

4-9-21 Nipponbashi, Naniwa-ku
Thurs–Tues 12pm–7pm
Osaka–Namba station, exit E9
[MAP p. 173 E3]

Fashion tells the story: one minute you're in, the next minute you're out – and the same goes for anime characters, toys, heroes, monsters and legends. When it's time to slink into the shadows, who will be there to make sure you shine again? Hero Gangu, that's who, a second-hand toy and character shop where crestfallen creatures, chewed-up champions, has-been heroines and passé pop-idols gather on overstuffed shelves to swap stories about the good old days. Aisle upon aisle of colourful pre-loved toys and models are ready to be loved again – by you. The stock here is staggering, ensuring hours of happy searching through retired robots and much-maligned monsters, in readiness to restore them to their former glory on a shelf at your place.

POCKET TIP

For fans of figurines, collectibles, vintage video games and model making, Naniwa-ku also has: Joshin Super Kids Land (4-12-4 Nipponbashi), Super Potato (3-8-18 Nipponbashi) and Yellow Submarine (3-8-23 Nipponbashi).

4 KUROMON ICHIBA MARKET

2 Chome-4-1 Nipponbashi,
Chuo-ku
[MAP p. 173 F2]

Established in 1902, Kuromon Ichiba Market is a covered arcade that celebrates Osaka's reputation as Japan's kitchen, with an intensely dedicated approach to local seafood. This strip caters to restauranteurs and home cooks, offering a dazzling array of fresh seafood in over 150 stalls. It draws the crowds: an estimated 25,000 people cram the market every day, raiding the various stands for the morning's haul – from oysters to a vast array of fish and a healthy dose of *what the heck is that?* ocean oddities. There are also eateries serving up the jewels of the sea in soup, ramen, curry, sushi and sashimi, crispy tempura and an array of tentacles and tendrils, grilled and skewered. Perennial Osaka favourites include fugu (puffer-fish), sea urchin and, of course, octopus, or those who prefer meat can join the queue for chunky just-grilled skewers of the renowned Kobe beef.

5 IBUKI COFFEE KUROMON

1-22-31 Nipponbashi, Chuo-ku
Mon–Sun 7am–7.45pm
Nipponbashi Station, exit 8 or 9
[MAP p. 173 F1]

One of Osaka's oldest and most-beloved coffee houses, Ibuki hides in the backstreets of Kuromon Ichiba Market (*see* p.41). A haunt of locals and creatives since 1934, the brown frontage with vintage typography looks curiously out of place, as the world has moved on while Ibuki has stayed the same. Up at 7am, they serve classic European coffee in white china cups, with sugar lumps on the side. Chandeliers hang from the ceiling and glass cabinets display curios. Old-timers sit in booths smoking and sipping coffee, while the younger generation meet in groups to write in journals or share a dessert. Order black coffee (served strong here), café au lait or drip-filter. The morning-set can be ordered before 11am: coffee, thick toast and a boiled egg, or a toasted tamago sando (egg sandwich). Relax with cake and coffee in the afternoon. For a touch of faded glamour, don't miss the coffee jelly, served in a martini glass, with a tiny stainless-steel pourer full of cream. Buy some coffee beans from next door, if you fancy taking a little of Osaka home.

6 NARUTO TAIYAKI HOMPO

2-1-1 Nanbanaka, Naniwa-ku
Mon–Sun 11am–10pm
[MAP p. 173 E2]

Follow the wafting aroma of baking and join the loose queue of Den Den town nerds, random salary men and out-of-towners. An oversized, brightly lit graphic sign featuring sweet potato and red beans announces this hole-in-the-wall dessert stand specialising in taiyaki – sea bream-shaped sweet pastries. Don't let the savoury nature of the pastry shape fool you – this is a sticky sweet delight. A few coins will buy you a piping hot, small but perfectly formed red bean or sweet potato-filled taiyaki – cooked right in front of you. Naruto have perfected the crispy-batter-to-gooey-filling ratio, which is why this store is so popular amongst locals. Also on offer is a tasty ball of light ice-cream sandwiched between two wafers. The atmosphere is lively with people spilling onto the street, standing around eating, talking and laughing. It is the perfect sugar hit after a long day of vintage toy shopping or retro gaming adventures.

SHINSAIBASHI & NAMBA

Prepare yourself for hours of shopping and taking photos in Shinsaibashi and Namba, effectively Osaka's central point, taking up a sizable portion of land, and featuring several of the city's major attractions. It's a stay-up-late precinct, noisy, hungry and visual, from the crush and colour of Dotonbori Shopping Street (*see* p. 57) and its rows of street food stalls (it's not called Japan's Kitchen for nothing), to the iconic, towering Glico Man sign (*see* p. 51) and oddball lion-headed Namba Yasaka Shrine (*see* p. 46). For the town that prides itself on humour and doesn't take itself too seriously, this area will have you smiling goofily at character signs on eateries, breakout street performances and rowdy, showy hawkers.

You won't go hungry, as eateries are everywhere and the same goes for bars and coffee joints. Head to Ajinoya (*see* p. 59) for Michelin-rated okonomiyaki (omelette pancake), trawl the bars in the Misono Building (*see* p. 61) and for a late-night ramen fix, head to Kinryu Ramen/Dotonbori (*see* p. 58). One thing is for sure, you're not in Tokyo or Kyoto now – Osaka has a rough and ready reputation and it doesn't mind a bit, and Shinsaibashi and Namba are right in the thick of the action.

→ *Dotonbori crazy signage*

SIGHTS

1. Namba Yasaka Shrine
2. Hozenji Temple
3. Namba Hatch
4. Glico Man sign

SHOPPING

5. Sennichimae Doguyasuji Shotengai
6. Shinsaibashi Daimaru
7. Eva Evam
8. Dotonbori Shopping Street

EATING & DRINKING

9. Kinryu Ramen Dotonbori
10. Ajinoya
11. Namba standing bars & drinking dens
12. Ura-Namba

1 NAMBA YASAKA SHRINE

2-9-19 Motomachi, Naniwa-ku
6641 1149
Mon–Sun 24 hrs
Osaka–Namba station, exit 6
[MAP p. 172 B3]

Constructed in 1975, we think the Lion's Head Shrine (Ema-Den) of Namba Yasaka is one of contemporary Osaka's most memorable moments – a monstrous stone lion head that brings good luck to students and workers but bad luck to anyone who gets a whiff of that lion breath. With most of the original buildings on the grounds now lost, the Namba Yasaka Shrine has made the most of rebuilding its spiritual base by creating a startling structure that pays homage to the original but adds a bold and comical edginess. The shrine is also a sakura (cherry blossom) hotspot during Hanami (cherry blossom season), with bursts of pink lending the frightening lion's head a friendlier look.

POCKET TIP

A fun festival takes place at the shrine on the third Sunday in January, where people test their strength in a massive tug-of-war competition. Join in, if you dare.

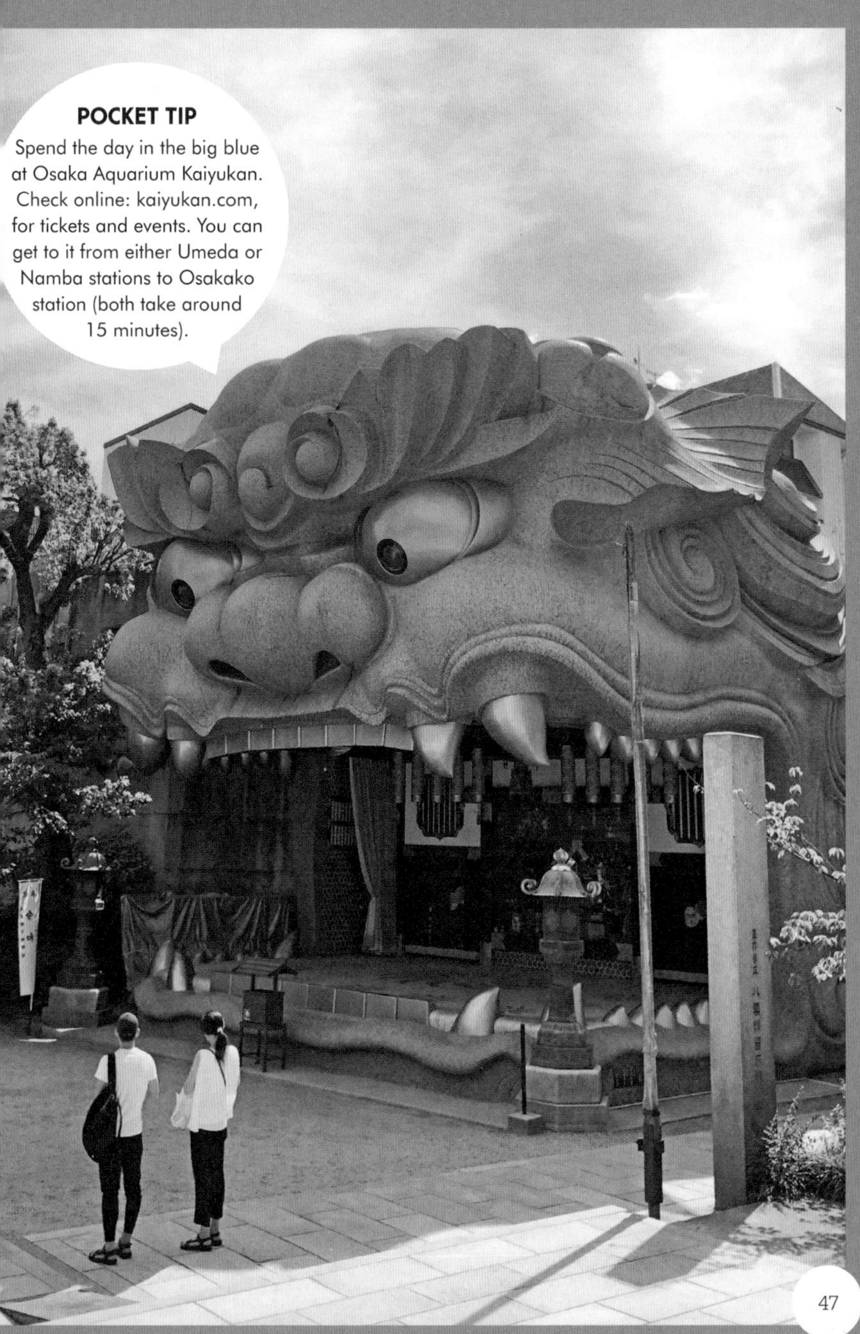

POCKET TIP

Spend the day in the big blue at Osaka Aquarium Kaiyukan. Check online: kaiyukan.com, for tickets and events. You can get to it from either Umeda or Namba stations to Osakako station (both take around 15 minutes).

2 HOZENJI TEMPLE

1-2-6 Namba, Chuo-ku
6211 4152
Mon–Sun 10am–10pm
Osaka–Namba station, exit B16, B18 or B20
[MAP p. 155 D4]

At Osaka's 'good luck' shrine, scoop up water to splash the statue of deity Fudomyoo (Mr Fudo) for good luck. Fudomyoo is a moss-covered yeti standing before a vessel filled with water with a ladle. This cherished temple stands as a bastion of calm on the outskirts of busy Dotonbori and it perfectly complements the old-meets-new, multi-faceted Ura–Namba area. It's a good early morning jump-off point, or head here after a day of shopping for a late evening of contemplation, when the stone and paper lamps are lit, creating an atmospheric glow. Paper lanterns are stacked together in groups and lanterns adorn the signage. The statue of Mr Fudo has been bringing good luck to the area for many years and now he can bring luck to you.

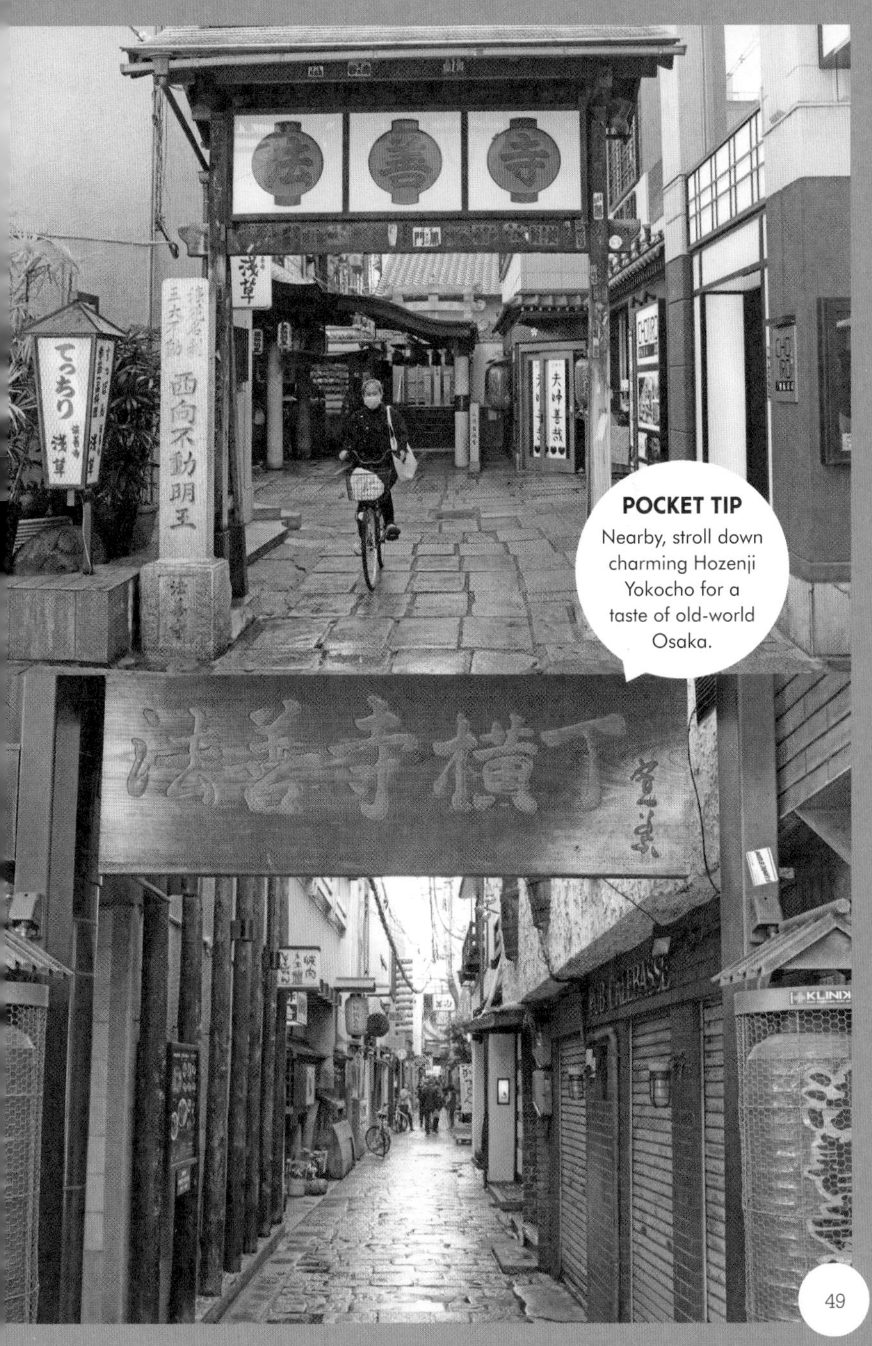

POCKET TIP

Nearby, stroll down charming Hozenji Yokocho for a taste of old-world Osaka.

3 NAMBA HATCH

1-3-1 Minatomachi, Naniwa-ku
4397 0572
www.namba-hatch.com
Hours vary
Osaka–Namba station,
Minatomachi River Place exit
[MAP p. 156 C4]

We think that Namba Hatch looks like a spaceship that landed in the '80s looking for youthful devotees and liked them so much that it decided to stay. Looming large on the Osaka–Namba skyline, the Hatch is retro-futurism, a pod-like entertainment venue that looks resplendent lit up at night on its perch next to the spaghetti-like major arterial roads of Minatomachi. It's an atmospheric sight reflected in the waters of the Dotonbori River. Namba Hatch holds 1500 people, easily one of Japan's largest entertainment halls. Set the controls for music and fun, with touring bands, playing jazz, rock, pop, hip hop, funk, you name it, bringing the stage to life and preparing Namba Hatch for lift-off. Check ahead and book online for events.

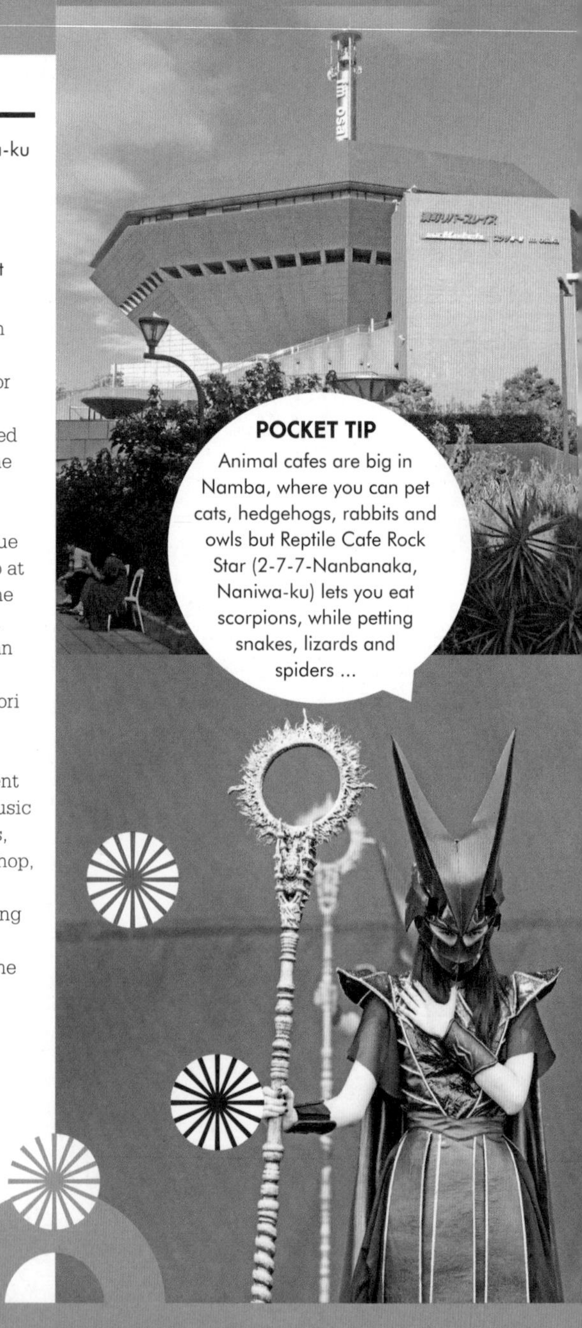

POCKET TIP

Animal cafes are big in Namba, where you can pet cats, hedgehogs, rabbits and owls but Reptile Cafe Rock Star (2-7-7-Nanbanaka, Naniwa-ku) lets you eat scorpions, while petting snakes, lizards and spiders ...

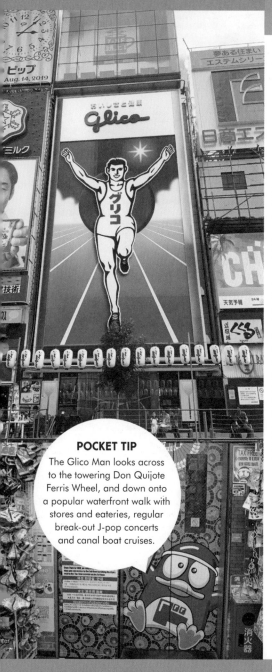

4 GLICO MAN SIGN

1-10-2 Dotonbori, Chuo-ku
6130 4208
Mon–Sun 24 hrs
Osaka–Namba station, exit 15A
[MAP p. 154 C2]

The athletic 33-metre-high (108 feet) Glico Man first burst through the tape in front position in 1935 and has since been frozen in time. He was a symbol of Glico (a Japanese confectionery company) and its winning attitude, but now has a new life as an icon of Osaka. The sign is altered for significant sporting events and is a popular meeting place. As a photo opportunity it is top-floor, a towering statement of glory, with the surrounding signs adding much to the allure, especially at night when it's one of Japan's spectacular neon-scapes. It also heralds your entrance into one of Osaka's busiest and most popular areas around crowded Ebisu Bridge spanning the Dotonbori Canal.

POCKET TIP

The Glico Man looks across to the towering Don Quijote Ferris Wheel, and down onto a popular waterfront walk with stores and eateries, regular break-out J-pop concerts and canal boat cruises.

5 SENNICHIMAE DOGUYASUJI SHOTENGAI

14-5 Nanbasennichimae,
Chuo-ku
6633 1423
Mon–Sun 10am–6pm
Osaka–Namba station, exit E9
[MAP p. 173 D2]

This 150-metre-long strip dealing almost exclusively in cooking supplies is often referred to as Kitchenware Street, and sometimes as the 'kitchen of a nation'. Once a pilgrimage trail between Hozenji Temple (*see* p. 48) and southern Shitennoji Temple (*see* p. 111), the strip has since been subject to several disasters, including a major fire in 1912 and bombing raids in 1945 during World War II. A shady black market history followed, but when things were cleaned up in the '50s, the street really took on a life of its own, becoming Osaka's premiere strip for homewares, kitchenware, kitchen utensils and restaurant supplies. Wanting to purchase a premium Japanese knife? This is the place to go. Cutlery, ceramics, noren curtains, plastic sample food, lucky cats, food signage and packaging – that's just for starters. Wander into any establishment and there will be something to enhance your kitchen or improve your cooking skills.

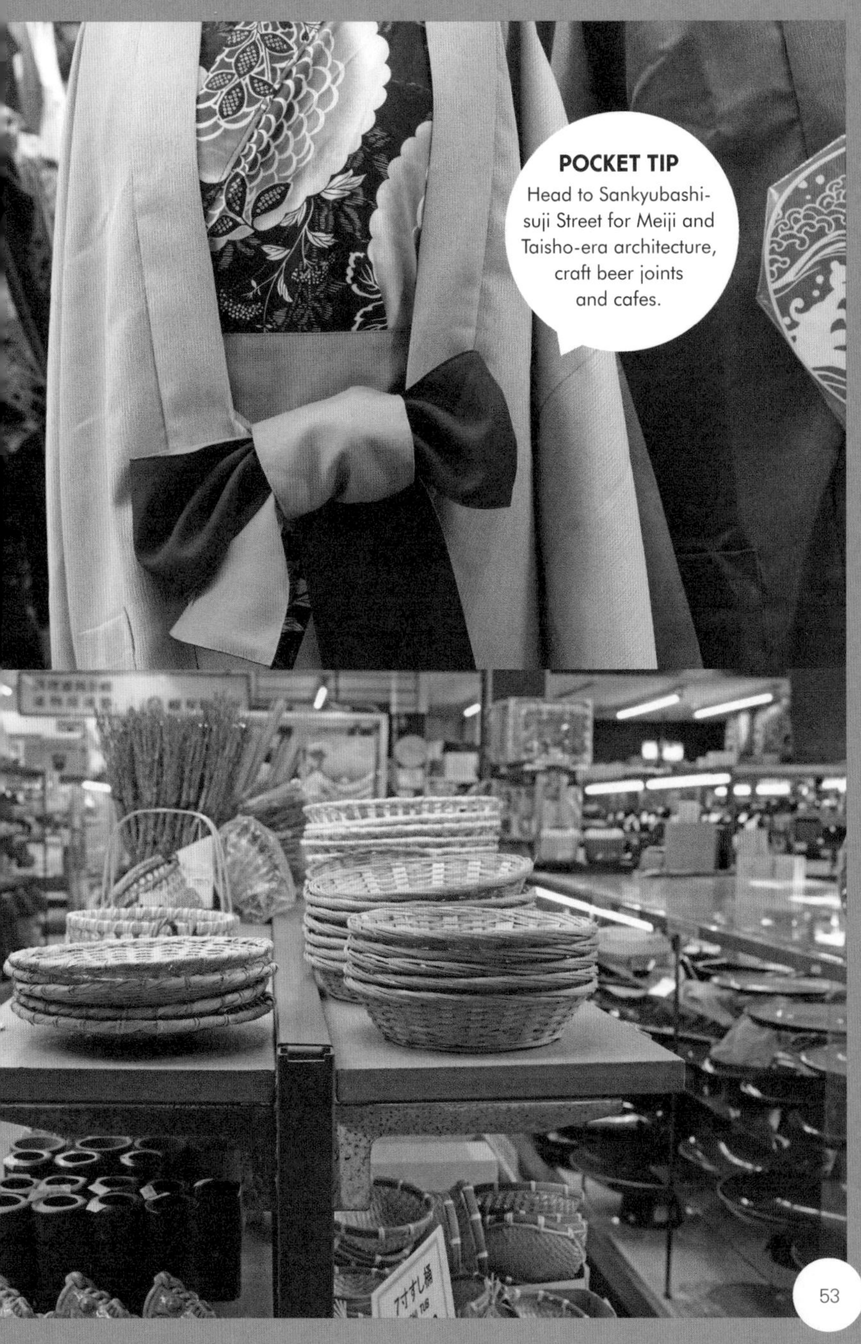

POCKET TIP

Head to Sankyubashi-suji Street for Meiji and Taisho-era architecture, craft beer joints and cafes.

6 SHINSAIBASHI DAIMARU

1-7-1 Shinsaibashisuji, Chuo-ku
6271 1231
Mon–Sun 10am–8.30pm
Shinsaibashi station, exit 6
[MAP p. 159 E2]

William Merril Vories, a missionary, teacher, architect and entrepreneur, built the neo-gothic monolith that houses the Shinsaibashi Daimaru department store. Take some photographs of the austere block and its lofty spire, an out-of-place bit of early Europe in the middle of Osaka. Inside, you'll find a choice selection of stores, with the middle levels being devoted to high-end fashion and homewares. Simple but chic Scandinavian 'coastal skincare' store **La Bruket** makes a rare Japanese appearance on the seventh floor – some select products use Japanese Hinoki oil. Other shops of interest include Japanese tea shop **Needle to Leaf**; **Ise Ebiya**, which showcases folk cotton craft from the Mie Prefecture; repurposed artisan kimono store **Nagamochiya**; and Buddhist bead, incense and altar supplier **Law Cloud Temple**. Kids will love the **Pokemon centre** on the ninth floor. As with every Daimaru store, the **Daimaru Food Hall** in the basement is exceptional.

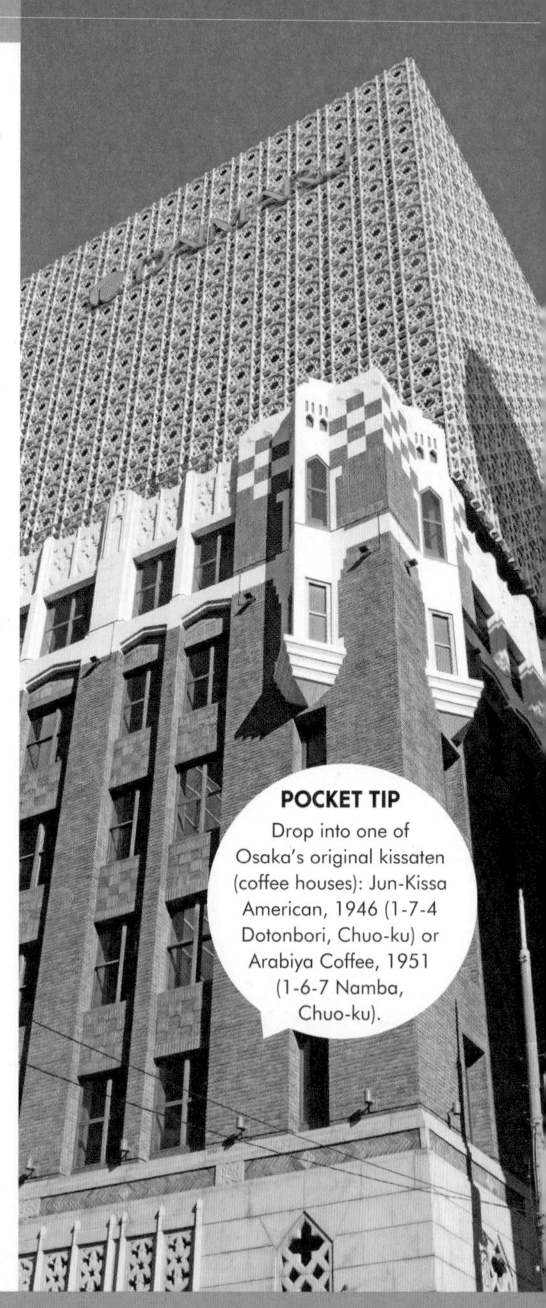

POCKET TIP

Drop into one of Osaka's original kissaten (coffee houses): Jun-Kissa American, 1946 (1-7-4 Dotonbori, Chuo-ku) or Arabiya Coffee, 1951 (1-6-7 Namba, Chuo-ku).

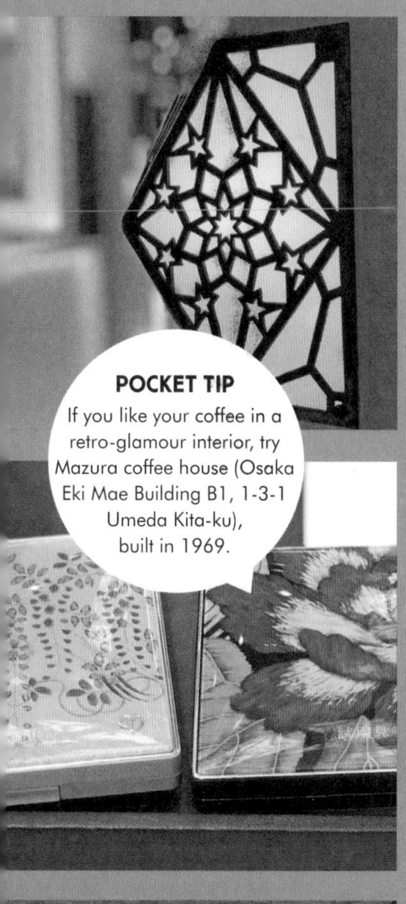

POCKET TIP

If you like your coffee in a retro-glamour interior, try Mazura coffee house (Osaka Eki Mae Building B1, 1-3-1 Umeda Kita-ku), built in 1969.

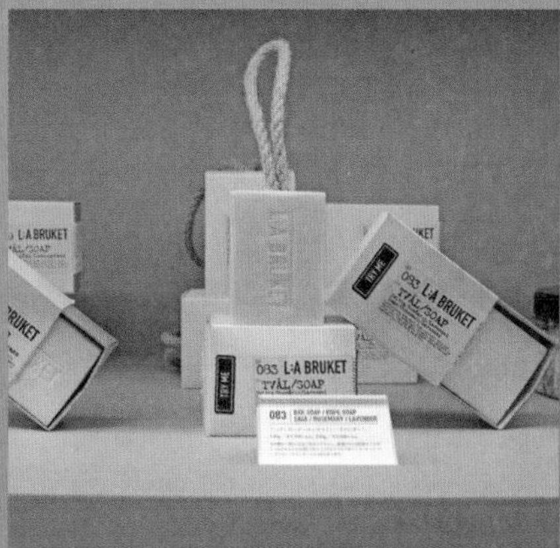

7 EVA EVAM

5F Takashimaya, 5-1-5 Namba, Chuo-ku
6632 9535
Sun–Thurs 10am–8pm, Fri–Sat 10am–8.30pm
Osaka–Namba station, exit E10
[MAP p. 172 C2]

Born from the Kondo Knit company, established in 1945, Eva Evam is a classic, stylish Japanese brand. Finding a piece here means finding an item of clothing that will be both your regular go-to for a breezy day and an informal evening out. The clothing is made from all natural fibres, including cashmere, wool and linen, with an eye to classic styles that aren't subject to the fluctuations of fashion. Predominantly a women's clothing and lifestyle store, they also make a small selection of thoughtful menswear in this small, open boutique on the fifth floor of **Takashimaya Department Store**. Eva Evam make a point of stressing that they want the item you buy not just to be special, but to be one of your favourite pieces. It's not hard with their relaxed and perfectly cut pieces; the ideal mid-point between beauty and wearability. The non-showy, muted colour palette adds to the allure of the Japanese chemistry, where the everyday meets the effortlessly stylish.

POCKET TIP

If you haven't shopped enough, and you love crowds, fashion and chain stores, hit the covered arcade Shinsaibashi Suji, which attracts over 60,000 shoppers a day.

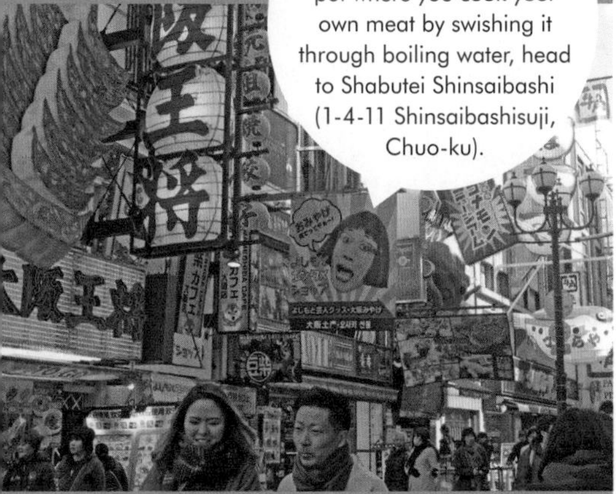

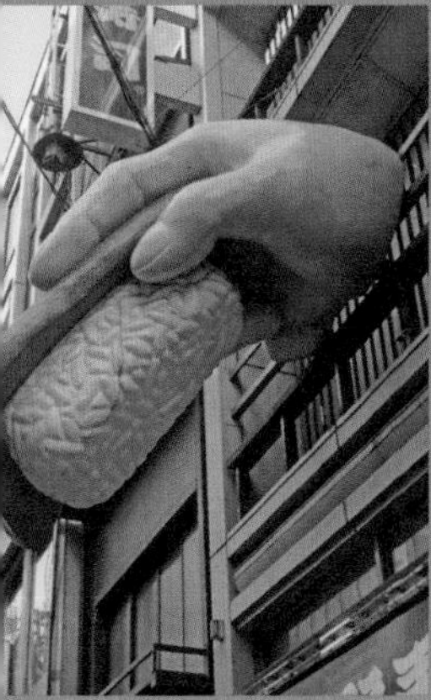

8 DOTONBORI SHOPPING STREET

[MAP p. 155 D3]

Rowdy, lively, manic – Dotonbori Shopping Street is the spirit of Osaka and Japan's 'kitchen'. It is one of Osaka's most recognisable sights, a brash, loud, outrageously colourful street that brings visitors flocking. It is Osaka on a plate, where you'll find the absurdly huge restaurant signs, including one of the famed giant fugu (puffer-fish, the other one is in Shinsekai), huge crabs and frightening dragons. There's always an egotistical restauranteur who'll happily put a giant plastic image of their own head out the front of their shop. You'll meet all manner of spruikers, taste-testers and cuddly creatures handing out flyers, enticing you into fun eateries. You might not make it inside though, as the street food stalls will probably get you first. It's a permanent festival – get amongst it and eat, jostle through crowds, snap pop colour photos and marvel at just how crazy a big city can get.

POCKET TIP

If you feel the need for shabu shabu, the hot-pot where you cook your own meat by swishing it through boiling water, head to Shabutei Shinsaibashi (1-4-11 Shinsaibashisuji, Chuo-ku).

9 KINRYU RAMEN DOTONBORI

1-7-26 Dotonbori, Chuo-ku
6211 6202
Mon–Sun 24 hrs
Osaka–Namba station, exit B20
[MAP p. 155 E3]

Why not set up an open kitchen in the middle of a street with a giant gold dragon prowling around the top? Kinryu Ramen is a messy and unpretentious Namba institution, with energy to burn. It serves two types of ramen: one with pork and one with extra pork. It doesn't scrimp on flavour, the tonkotsu ramen (based on pork bones boiled for several hours) has a hint of sesame oil and plenty of bite. It's the perfect meal for lunch, dinner or after a few too many in the wee hours of the morning, when waifs and strays can be found standing at the bar, sitting on the ground or perched in the middle of the street soaking up a night of drinking with a restorative bowl of hot broth, pork and noodles. It's pure theatre inside the open kitchen, as well as outside on the street. Just like a dragon it's fast and furious – a good ramen with added crazy at a rock-bottom price.

POCKET TIP

Mattari Purin (1-9-17 Dotonbori, Chuo-ku) is a retro hole-in-the-wall dessert joint with wonderful vintage signage that sells chilled custard 'pudding cups'.

POCKET TIP

90-year-old Meijiken is a must if you are a fan of omaraisu (omurice) in an old-school setting. (1-5-32 Shinsaibashisuji, Chuo-ku).

10 AJINOYA

1-7-16 Namba, Chuo-ku
6211 0713
Tues–Fri 12pm–10pm, Sat–Sun 11.30am–10.45pm
Osaka–Namba station, exit 14
[MAP p. 154 C3]

If you want to go where the locals go for okonomiyaki (savoury omelette), then Ajinoya is the place. Established in 1965, Ajinoya manages to add some real delicacy to the humble omelette with attitude. Light and fluffy batter and fresh ingredients (including ham, prawn, squid, various seasonal vegetables, noodles and egg) are lovingly put together in front of you. As Ajinoya put it, 'it feels like a time slip to the old okonomiyaki shop in the old town'. The quality earned them a Bib Gourmand in the Michelin Guide, just short of a star, but indicating affordability and highly recommended by the best of the best taste testers. Their sweet sauce and 'special mix' topping have also garnered fans across the world and can be ordered online (ajinoya.shop-pro.jp). Take it from us, a 50-seat venue with a constant turnover of rowdy, hungry customers makes for a lively atmosphere. Expect queues at any time but we suggest getting there at opening time (you'll still have to line up but they'll take your order while you wait). It's cash only.

11 NAMBA STANDING BARS & DRINKING DENS

Osaka–Namba station, exit 25

Cross the Shinebisu bridge, bid a fond farewell to the bright lights and head into quieter streets. Here old friends gather in longstanding izakaya (pubs with small-plate food), groups catch up in shoebox-sized standing bars and locals gather to celebrate the weekend with a drink or two in some of Osaka's oldest and most atmospheric drinking dens. We love this mysterious in-between world, not quite Dotonbori, not quite Namba. Order yakitori skewers, grilled meat dishes and tasty small plates, while you watch people drift past the window on the way to the next rowdy bar or food haunt. Drop into **Tsurugi** (2-2-13 Dotonbori, Chuo-ku), **Oui** bar (2-4-11 Nishishinsaibashi, Chuo-ku) or the enticingly named **Sexmachine** (2-4-4 Dotonbori, Chuo-ku). For a more contemporary bar head to **Craft Beer Gulp** (2-4-6 Namba, Chuo-ku). If you get super loose, round the night off at **Onion Stage Karaoke** (2-4-1 Namba, Chuo-ku) and belt out a few heartbreakers.

POCKET TIP

Snap some shots of the oddball Namba Hips (1-8-16 Namba, Chuo-ku) building, then head inside for ten storeys of fun – karaoke, game parlours and even a golf course.

12 URA-NAMBA

[MAP p. 173 E2]

Faded chintzy glamour, cheaper rent and reinvention equals one of Osaka's most interesting nightlife hubs. Ura-Namba (the 'private face' of Namba) is a network of warrens, alleys and lanes to the south-east of Osaka–Namba station. Once an area with a proud history of the performing arts (infamous comedy theatre **Grand Kagetsu** was here), as well as furniture makers, restorers and later, dancing and drinking, the area fell on hard times when the economic bubble burst in the late '80s. The retro-tinged maze of discovery and intrigue gets better after a drink or two. The **Misono Building** (2-3-9 Sennichimae, Chuo-ku), a neon-lit '50s hub turned '80s hangover is a good place to bar-hop. Walk up the stately spiral ramp to a floor full of messy corridors and doors that hide tiny bars and eateries. The second floor is a dark carnival of theme bars full of character and whimsy. It's a great place to head to for a (very) late-night drinking adventure.

POCKET TIP

If you're fond of a tipple, head into Bar Masuda (2-3-11 Shinsaibashi Suji, Chuo-ku) for choice cocktails or to Bar Country (5-34 Souemoncho, Chuo-ku) or Bar Freedom (1-6-14 Sennichimae, Chuo-ku) for a huge selection of whisky.

MINAMISENBA & HONMACHI

With manic Shinsaibashi and Namba to the south and bustling Osaka–Umeda station (*see* p. xii) to the north, we look to Minamisenba and Honmachi as our little corner of peace and quiet, where the Japanese aesthetic for intricate beauty and attention to detail thrives. Places here are less crowded, more relaxed and decidedly more genteel. Streets and shops have a more intimate feel, sidewalk cafes and Osaka designer stores line the streets, and a local craft and artisan feel takes over. Cafes like Wad Omotenashi (*see* p. 68) and sophisticated eateries like Tofu Sorano Minamisemba (*see* p. 72) set the scene.

The precinct's arts and culture are celebrated in shrines and museums, and more than one Osaka secret can be found hidden among the lanes that offshoot from the open thoroughfares. Tea-lovers can travel a bit further north for the Yuki Museum of Art (*see* p. 64), dedicated to the Japanese art of tea, while Mochisho Shizuku Shinmachi (*see* p. 70) elevates the wagashi (Japanese sweet) into an art form. A burgeoning new, vibrant Osaka is staking a claim here, with young creatives paving the way, deliberately kicking against the bold and brash reputation of the surrounding precincts.

→ *Beautiful display at Mochisho Shizuku Shinmachi*

SIGHTS
1. Yuki Museum of Art
2. Goryo-Jinja Shrine

SHOPPING
3. Tokyu Hands
4. Acorn Vintage

SHOPPING & EATING
5. Wad Omotenashi
6. Mochisho Shizuku Shinmachi

EATING
7. Torisoba Zagin Niboshi
8. Tofu Ryori Sorano Minamisemba

1 YUKI MUSEUM OF ART

3-3-9 Hiranomachi, Chuo-ku
6203 0188
Tues–Sun 10am–4pm
Yodoyabashi station, exit 11
[MAP p. 163 F3]

Opened in 1987, this one-floor museum has a permanent collection that will thrill anyone obsessed with Japanese tea and tea rituals, and intrigue anyone wanting to know more about the history and art of tea. Teiichi Yuki, founder of Osaka's famous Kiccho Kaiseki restaurant, put together the beautiful collection of tea ceremony ceramics, utensils and tools, collected over a 50-year period, housed in the space where the actual restaurant was located. Memorable pieces include antiques from the Nara and Edo-eras – among them are 13 'Important Cultural properties', including special tea ceremony items, like the Shino Chawan 'Breath of fresh air' bowl; pages from the poetry collections of Ishiyamagire and Kokin Wakashu; and some Oribe Yoho Tebachi (Oribe square bowl with handle). The spaces are set up to mimic actual tea ceremony rooms and if all of this is your cup of tea, you can partake in special tea ceremonies in a traditional tatami room.

2 GORYO-JINJA SHRINE

4-4-3 Awajimachi, Naniwa-ku
6231 5041
Mon–Sun 7am–5pm
Hommachi station, exit 2
[MAP p. 163 E3]

This 9th century Meiji-era Shinto Shrine is fronted by an impressive vermillion tori gate. A small but important shrine, Goryo-Jinja is the protector of the Umeda and Sonezaki areas, and a prime Osakan sacred site where many festivals are held. It's also a major spot for sakura (cherry blossom) viewing. We lit our own lanterns at the **Autumn Lantern Festival** and placed them around the shrine – a very atmospheric experience. Several other festivals are held at Goryo-Jinja, including the important Yasoshima festival, **Setsubun**, as well as the summer festival and the new year's festival. Many gods of education and agriculture are enshrined at Goryo. The Kami Gyusha, (cowshed) enshrines a cow statue with healing powers. Just touch the place of your illness and run your hand over the cow, and wait for a miracle.

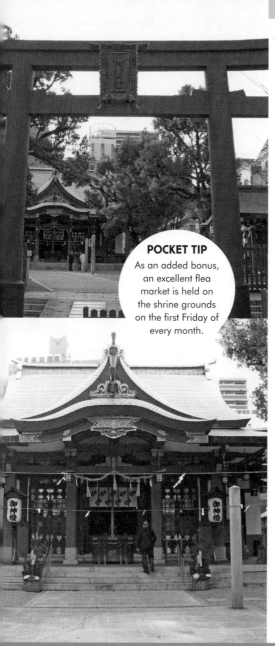

POCKET TIP

As an added bonus, an excellent flea market is held on the shrine grounds on the first Friday of every month.

3 TOKYU HANDS

3-4-12 Minamisenba, Chuo-ku
6243 3111
Mon–Sun 10am–9pm
Shinsaibashi station, exit 2
[MAP p. 161 F4]

This rambling, messy DIY wonderland is perfect for Osaka, a 'do-it-yourself' city – if ever there was one. With a sometimes shambolic collection of thingummy-jigs, and bits and bobs over many floors, you can easily drop an afternoon here. You'll find homewares, health products, amazing orthotics, travelware, lights, electronics, an incredible bag selection, bicycle tool kits, and other handy 'why didn't I think of that?' inventions. However, it's the craft and handy fix-it fanatics that will go crazy for washi (paper) tapes, stationery, tool kits, home maintenance products, screws, nails, cleaning products and so much more. Products also reflect the season – there are ways to keep warm and cool, keep you safe from 'humidity hair', keep you dry when it rains and keep dry skin moisturised and hydrated in summer. You'll go into Tokyu Hands with the intention of looking around and emerge many hours later with bags full of Japan-made products that will change your life.

POCKET TIP

After exhausting yourself at Tokyu Hands, pop in for a coffee or juice at Saturdays NYC (4-13-22 Minamisenba, Chuo-ku) and scour their collection of clothes, accessories and … surfboards.

4 ACORN VINTAGE

4-9-5 Minamisenba, Chuo-ku
6243 3111
Mon–Sun 12pm–8pm
Shinsaibashi station, exit 3
[MAP p. 161 D2]

Acorn Vintage is for the shopper who knows their own personal style and is on the hunt for very particular shapes, colours and fit. Stylishly packaged, it masquerades as a designer fashion store, but everything in here is pre-loved or pre-worn and waiting for a new home. The emphasis is on American classics, college wear, street wear and trainers, with a heavy leaning towards denim, in particular Levis 501 and 505. If you are looking to kit yourself out in some American-made clothing, sort through their racks of U.S. navy and army surplus. Adventurers might find some more rugged apparel among their favourite selection of brands. Baseball tops, sneakers and even second-hand leather jackets will help you put together a look that has your friends asking: 'where did you get that?'

POCKET TIP

After you've sorted your outfit at Acorn, pop into nearby Especial Records (4-9-2 Minamisenba, Chuo-ku) for a great selection of rare groove, soul, jazz and funk vinyl, and a set of their cool personalised turntable slip mats.

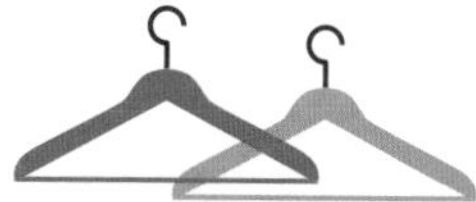

5 WAD OMOTENASHI

4-9-3 Motomachi, Naniwa-ku
4708 3616
Mon–Sun 10am–7pm
Shinsaibashi station, exit 3
[MAP p. 161 D2]

Wad's small and perfect tearoom is a highlight of every trip we take to Osaka. Finding the tiny sign and climbing the stairs is all part of the reveal. Moss-filled terrariums hang before wafting noren curtains. Staff float around the room in immaculate linen uniforms. Low-hanging lights, warm woods and repurposed furniture complete Wad's take on a traditional tea ceremony room. Omotenashi means hospitality, and your experience will be a masterclass in sophisticated subtlety. The menu is concise, a curated selection of tea from Wazuka-cho (Kyoto). Cold and hot matcha, sencha and hojicha are served as a set with wagashi (Japanese sweets). When you order the matcha, staff let you choose a handmade vessel before whisking the tea. The kakigori (shaved-ice dessert) is a must, we like to order it with red bean and syrup extras. Wad also has a gallery curating their favourite artists from around the country and you can buy expertly chosen ceramics displayed in the tearoom, like artworks in a gallery – simply beautiful.

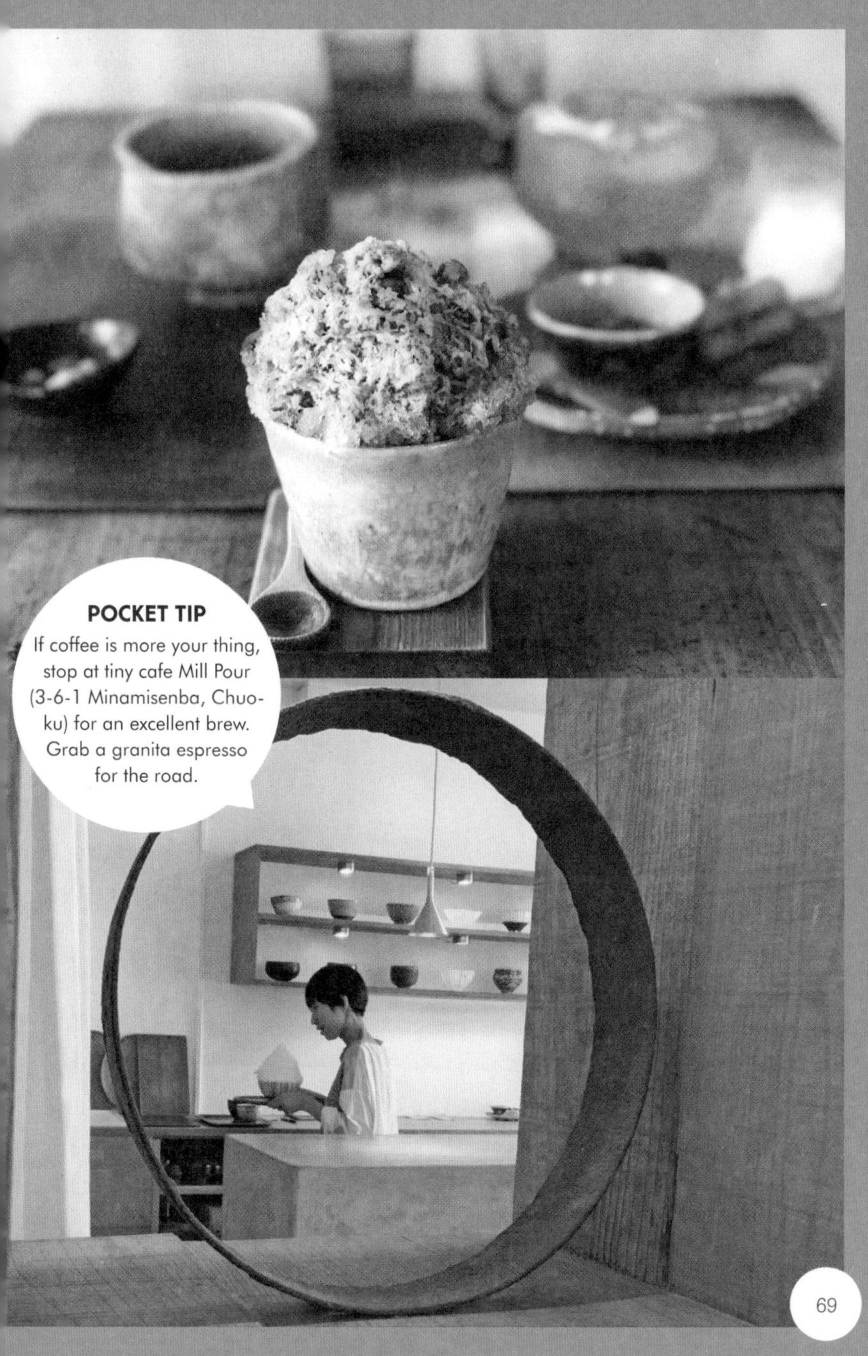

POCKET TIP

If coffee is more your thing, stop at tiny cafe Mill Pour (3-6-1 Minamisenba, Chuo-ku) for an excellent brew. Grab a granita espresso for the road.

6 MOCHISHO SHIZUKU SHINMACHI

1F Shinmachi House, 1-17-17 Shinmachi, Nishi-ku
6536 0805
Mon–Sun 10.30am–7pm
Nishi Ohashi station, exit 2
[MAP p. 160 A2]

Mochi is a rice-flour sweet, usually with a red bean filling, and when done just right, it's a visual delight and one of the most delicious things you can eat. Mochisho Shizuku Shinmachi turns mochi into an art form. The architectural building with big glass panels reveals a modernist interior, with a large bench at one end to eat mochi and sip tea. At the other end intricate mochi is displayed in a gallery-like setting, lined-up like delicate jewels in display cases on the counter. It's all so beautiful you almost feel like you want to ask who the artist is. A must-try is the 'deconstructed' kakigori (shaved-ice dessert). Mochi pudding also sees us returning for more. Take some away to enjoy on your travels (always remember to check the use-by date). The simple, streamlined packaging hides the fact that you are carrying a bag full of gleaming gems.

7 TORISOBA ZAGIN NIBOSHI

3-9-6 Minamisenba, Chuo-ku
6244 1255
Tues–Sun 11am–10.30pm
Osaka–Namba station, exit 6
[MAP p. 161 E2]

Join the queue of mainly female clientele (drawn in by a lighter, creamier style of ramen, perhaps) on a quiet backstreet, for one of the best ramen experiences you'll have in Osaka. Order at the machine outside (there is an English menu available) to select your ramen in advance. This is also a good chance to choose ramen extras, like ginger or smoked egg. Once inside, the long eight-seater-counter is darkly lit, with down lighting illuminating a row of jars, like a vintage apothecary store, crammed with many types of dried fish. The secret here is the creamy chicken and sardine broth, which they claim achieves umami, the 'fifth taste' of sweet, sour, bitter and salty. Slices of chicken and pork sit next to an artfully presented tangle of deep fried burdock root, capping off the delicious flavour. The small but well thought-out menu also includes fried chicken and an Osaka favourite: 'beef sushi'. The price points are low, the staff are friendly and the area is perfect for a post-ramen stroll.

8 TOFU RYORI SORANO MINAMISEMBA

4-5-6 Minamikyuhojimachi,
Chuo-ku
6120 0644
Mon–Sat 5–10.20pm,
Sun 5–9.50pm
Homachi station, exit 15
[MAP p. 161 D1]

This is a favourite place of ours to visit in Osaka, because its vegetarian food is so expertly done (they also offer a few dishes for their meat-eating friends). The venue is chic and intimate, a designer cave of light woods and crisp white walls with a soaring vaulted ceiling; it looks imposing but this is a very relaxed and cosy eatery. Tofu Ryori Sorano presents the very best way to eat tofu – fresh and without additives. They use premium soybeans from Hokkaido, worked into various intriguing and delicious dishes. The real star of the show however, is the tofu that is 'created' at your table while you wait: a beautiful jewel box of curd heated over a stone pot until it slowly forms into the freshest tofu you could possibly have. Drizzled with soy, it would convert any die-hard meat eater. For lovers of the soybean, try the soy milk cocktail – one of our favourites. As an added bonus, it won't break the budget.

POCKET TIP

Issey Miyake Semba (4-11-28 Minamisemba, Chuo-ku) is a gorgeous store and the only place in Osaka to carry multiple Issey labels.

AMERIKAMURA, HORIE & NISHISHINSAIBASHI

Amerikamura, affectionately known by locals as Amermura, boasts the title of being the birthplace of modern American street culture in Japan, an interesting counterpoint to the country's deep and spiritual history. In true Osakan style, it has somehow moulded, changed and reinvented itself as a hybrid of the best (or questionable parts) of both cultures. Trainer shops, fast food and coffee take up much of the real estate here. Set within big brash Shinsaibashi, it has forged its own path and become a destination for youth culture in its own right. It encompasses two noisy, messy and colourful blocks crammed with vintage clothing, with numerous famous vintage stores like First (*see* p. 80) and Stay Gold (*see* p. 80), pre-loved vinyl stores like Time Bomb (*see* p. 79) and King Kong Records (*see* p. 78), all punctuated by interesting and relaxed street food stalls (and even more interesting and relaxed people). Amermura features some standout cafes and Lilo Coffee Roasters (*see* p. 84) makes the perfect pick-me-up, while live house Big Cat (*see* p. 79) is the perfect wind-down.

To the west, Horie is just as chilled out, but more upmarket almost like Amermura's big sister, with a plethora of independent design stores and cool coffee houses, like Adam Et Rope Biotop (*see* p. 82) and Streamer Coffee (*see* p. 84) dotting the labyrinthine streets and lanes. Perfect for a Sunday stroll, Amermura and Horie's independent spirits and non-chain store aesthetic are havens amidst the excesses of Shinsaibashi and Namba.

→ *One of the many colourful streets of Amerikamura*

SIGHTS
1. Street art & signage
2. Triangle Park

SHOPPING
3. Local music vibes
4. Time Bomb Records
5. Vintage shopping in Amerikamura
6. Orange Street
7. Alice on Wednesday

EATING & DRINKING
8. Lilo Coffee Roasters
9. Hokkyokusei Shinsaibashi
10. Westwood Bakers
11. Yaoya-to Gohan Shimizu
12. Kogaryu Takoyaki
13. Café Ori Ori

1 STREET ART & SIGNAGE

It might not seem a big deal, as murals are popular all over the world, but in Japan street art is usually washed away as soon as it goes up – Amermura makes an exception. Street art graces many of the walls of this precinct and it is complex and colourful, with all kinds of people lining up to admire the art and to snap pictures. Local artist Seitaro Kuroda's *Peace on Earth* (1983) features a giant feathery figure that commands your attention and takes over a whole wall in the area's south-east corner. Don't just peruse the walls, look up to admire the area's signature creative lampposts. There are three different types of stick-figure robots that stalk the area holding up street lamps and shop signs. The poles, set up in 2013, are covered in designs and paintings created by local artists. As an added bonus and a nod to the area's roots, there is a (much smaller) Statue of Liberty as well.

POCKET TIP

Head to Horie store Crackers (1-23-4 Kitahirie, Nishi-ku), where the local street art is printed onto streetwear.

2 TRIANGLE PARK

2-18-5 Nishishinsaibashi, Chuo-ku
6212 2264
Mon–Sun 24 hours
Shinsaibashi station, exit 7
[MAP p. 158 C3]

Also known as Mitsu or Sankaku Park, Triangle Park is a small urban amphitheatre, a concreted plot of land on a triangle wedge (hence the name) on the most manic corner of Amermura. A popular meeting spot and triangular catwalk for outrageous fashion parading, the 'park' is also a family hangout and the perfect place to enjoy some people-watching. Akin to Tokyo's Harajuku, the 'kids' gather here to see who can outfreak who – a 'look at me' fest that visitors are drawn to. As a result, it has become home to one of the world's biggest and most outrageous Halloween parties. A focal point for crowds, the park has become known as a popular hangout for comedians, where artists pre-trial their latest performances before a keen audience.

3 LOCAL MUSIC VIBES

In the heart of Amermura, you'll find a wealth of vinyl records stores and live-music venues. **King Kong Records** (B1 Shinsaibashi Big Step, 1-6-14 Nishishinsaibashi, Chuo-ku), is in the **Big Step** youth department store complex and doesn't monkey around (sorry I had to say it) – sifting through their racks you'll come up against metal, soundtracks, funk, soul, pop, rock, punk and disco. **Rare Groove** (1-9-28 Nishishinsaibashi Chuo-ku) is a must for DJs, you'll find a mix of soul, gospel, disco and house. **Root Down Records** (5F, 1-10-10-33 Nishishinsaibashi Chuo-ku), specialises in hip hop, funk, disco, soul, jazz and reggae. **Maru Ka Batsu** (1-5-2 Kitahorie Nishi-ku), dabbles more in progressive rock, industrial, J-pop's and indies, a mish-mash of sounds that should see most crate-diggers finding some real gems. Also try **Flake Records** (1-11-9 Minamihorie Nishi-ku) and **Groovenut** (2-17-13 Nishishinsaibashi Chuo-ku). Grab a drink or dinner at **Safari Izakaya** (1-9-16 Nishishinsaibashi Chuo-ku), before or after your adventure.

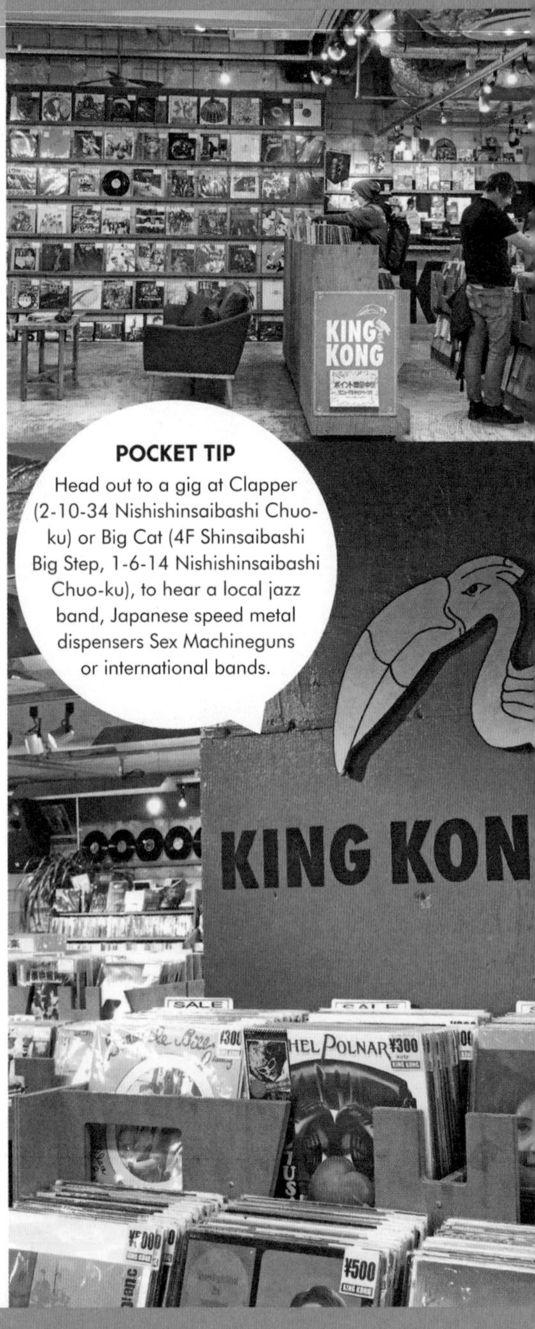

POCKET TIP

Head out to a gig at Clapper (2-10-34 Nishishinsaibashi Chuo-ku) or Big Cat (4F Shinsaibashi Big Step, 1-6-14 Nishishinsaibashi Chuo-ku), to hear a local jazz band, Japanese speed metal dispensers Sex Machineguns or international bands.

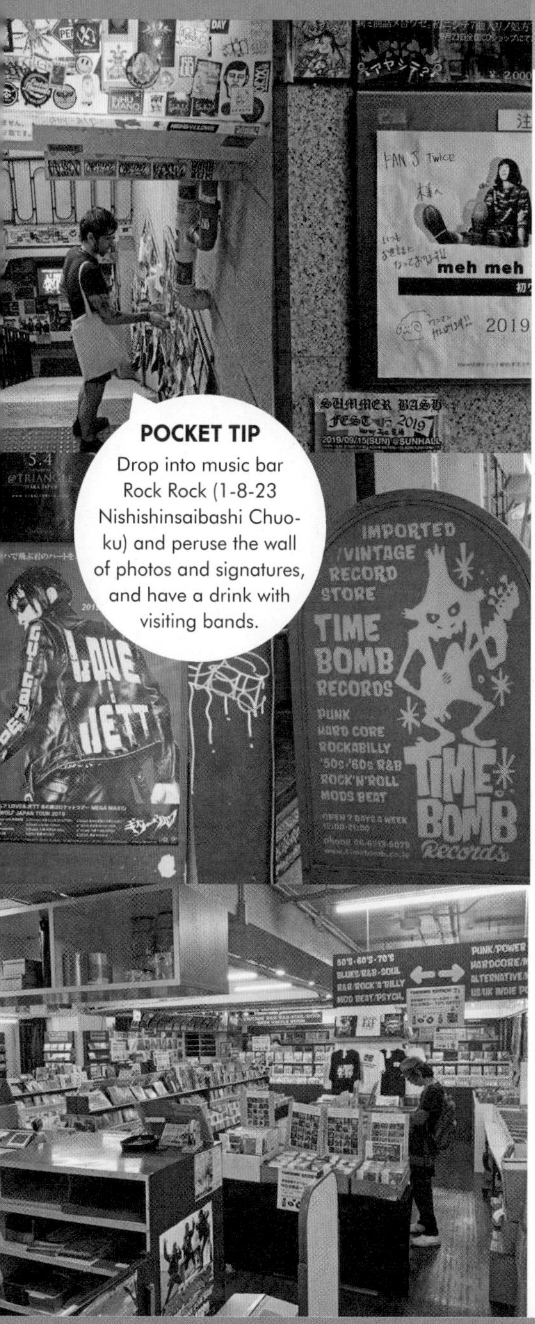

POCKET TIP

Drop into music bar Rock Rock (1-8-23 Nishishinsaibashi Chuo-ku) and peruse the wall of photos and signatures, and have a drink with visiting bands.

4 TIME BOMB RECORDS

Sun-Bowl B1, 2-9-28,
Nishishinsaibashi, Chuo-ku
6213 5079
www.timebomb.co.jp
Mon–Sun 12pm–9pm
Shinsaibashi station, exit 7
[MAP p. 157 E1]

Be careful, Time Bomb Records could go off at any moment! A two-room underground bunker beneath the Sun Bowl Building (look up for the massive bowling pin) is plastered in posters, club flyers and record sleeves and sells the latest in metal, punk, goth, gloom and doom (although we saw some Abba records so it's safe to assume that they have a broad reach). Outside, the street is sedate, nearly cute, but you'll hear the dirge and drone of the underworld beckoning you to turn the corner and descend into hell – or a kind of heaven for vinyl record collectors. The range is extensive and will give you hours of happy bin flipping (keep a sad face on, though). They also sell online, with good English, so if their leaning towards hardcore, punk and industrial sinks your boat, you always have Time Bomb's eclectic but passionate selection at your fingertips.

5 VINTAGE SHOPPING IN AMERIKAMURA

Amerikamura is known for many things but top of the list are the vintage clothing stores. Any up-cycle adventurer will find themselves in heaven as they sift through racks of second-generation clothing. The stock is mostly American import wear from the last thirty years with some Japanese labels thrown into the mix. **First** (1-5-16 Nishishinsaibashi, Chuo-ku) lays claim to being the 'first' vintage store in the ku (ward) so it's a good place to start. Other shops that have an extensive or well-sourced mix of vintage clothing include: **Vivie Vintage** (1-9-16 Nishishinsaibashi, Chuo-ku); **Kinji Used Clothing** (1-6-14 Nishishinsaibashi, Chuo-ku); **Pigsty** (1-7-14 Nishishinsaibashi, Chuo-ku); **Stay Gold** (1-8-19 Nishishinsaibashi, Chuo-ku); **Ducktail** (1-9-21 Nishishinsaibashi, Chuo-ku) and **Tunnel** (3F, 1-6-22 Nishishinsaibashi, Chuo-ku). However, singling out vintage stores in Amerikamura can be a fool's errand, as they pop up as practically every second or third shop. It's one of the highest concentrations we've seen anywhere in Japan, so vintage hunters make sure you make the most of it.

POCKET TIP

Cat lovers should slink over to Neko no Jikan (2 Chome-17-10 Nishishinsaibashi, Chuo-ku), the first cat cafe in Japan, which opened in 2004.

POCKET TIP

Retro game bar Space Station (2 Chome-13-3 Nishishinsaibashi, Chuo-ku) is both a bar and nostalgic game arcade.

6 ORANGE STREET

7 Minamihorie, Nishi-ku
Mon–Sun, hours vary
Yotsubashi station, exit 5
[MAP p. 156 C1, 158 A4]

Orange Street is a gentrified fashion and interiors strip that draws the weekend shoppers in droves. Your starting point is the huge vivid signpost blooming with illustrated oranges, proudly proclaiming the Orange Street name (in English). Not far from here you'll find **Adam Et Rope Biotop's** (1-16-1 Minamihorie Nishi-ku) Osaka base, a stylish and picturesque two-storey cafe and concept store, overgrown with lush greenery and plant life. Stop in for a coffee, and browse the clothing and homewares. Familiar semi-luxe stores dot the street and can be found in connecting alleys and lanes, such as stylish French label **A.P.C.** (1-16-1 Minamihorie, Nishi-ku); designer streetware and sneaker store **Supreme** (1-9-8 Minamihorie, Nishi-ku); brand megastore **Five Star** (1-16-15 Minamihorie Nishi-ku); **Bape** (1-19-3 Minamihorie Nishi-ku) and **Journal Standard Furniture** (1-16-19 Minamihorie Nishi-ku.

POCKET TIP

Orange Street is still home to some true relics of the past: pre-war antique and interior shops from a time when the street was famous for furniture.

7 ALICE ON WEDNESDAY

2-12-25 Nishishinsaibashi, Chuo-ku
6211 6506
Mon–Sun 11am–7.30pm
Shinsaibashi station, exit 7
[MAP p. 157 D2]

Eat me, drink me, you'll have to shrink down like Alice in Wonderland to fit into a tiny doorway that magically appeared one day on a wall in Amermura. Alice on Wednesday has a front door that is most definitely a selling point: a cute little archway that leads you into a magical emporium of Alice ephemera. The room is styled in Victorian gothic gloom with darkly painted walls, candles and low chandeliers. Shop a range of Cheshire Cat, the White Rabbit's pocket watch or 'eat me' brooches, plus snacks, cakes, ribbons, bows and all manner of merchandise of all-things-Alice. It's super-cute fun and, dare we say, it is a 'wonderland' of treasures. It's Japan's take on the classic novel, so in true Alice fashion there are surprises around every dimly-lit corner. You'd have to be a Mad Hatter not to step inside.

POCKET TIP

Get out of the city for a spell and head to The Wizarding World of Harry Potter. Check online: usj.co.jp, for tickets and events. You can get to it from either Osaka–Umeda or Namba stations to Universal City station (both take around 15 minutes).

8 LILO COFFEE ROASTERS

1-10-28 Nishishinsaibashi,
Chuo-ku
6227 8666
Mon–Sun 11am–11pm
Yotsubashi station, exit 3
[MAP p. 158 C1]

Osaka took its time joining the coffee revolution. Early adopter (even though it's just over two years young), Lilo Coffee Roasters features nearly 20 different types of single-origin beans sourced worldwide. The tiny room with posters and signs covering the walls, flyers on shelves and blackboards filling you in on the best bean buys, is likely to be full of queuing coffee enthusiasts. Lilo has become very popular and is placed perfectly on the edge of Amerikamura. The coffee is excellent, perch yourself outside on one of the benches and people-watch vintage or vinyl hunters as they slink down the street. Buy a T-shirt, tote bag or some take-away beans, then get hopped up on caffeine before heading into **Village Vanguard** (1-10-28 Nishishinsaibashi, Chuo-ku) next door for some crazy purchases.

POCKET TIP

Streamer Coffee (1-10-19 Nishishinsaibashi, Chuo-ku) is just a few stops down the road. Around the corner is Lilo Coffee Kissa (2-7-25 Nishishinsaibashi, Chuo-ku), Lilo's new store in the retro-style of a classic Japanese coffee house.

9 HOKKYOKUSEI SHINSAIBASHI

2-7-27 Nishishinsaibashi, Chuo-ku
6211 7829
Mon–Fri 11.30am–10pm, Sat–Sun 11am–10pm
Osaka–Namba station, exit B6
[MAP p. 157 E3]

There is a constant push and pull between omuraisu (rice-filled omelette) houses in Japan – who was first and who invented the dish? Tokyo or Osaka? General consensus puts the genesis in Ginza Tokyo at Renga-tei at the turn of the 20th century, but there's no doubt that Hokkyokusei here in Osaka has a legitimate claim to the title, given that there are various types and styles of omuraisu and a history that has been obscured over time. Hokkyokusei was established in 1922 and hasn't changed a whole lot since then – always a good sign. The authentic machiya (traditional wooden townhouse), with its wooden facade, noren curtains and tatami mats, plus the delicious recipes and machine ordering system, will immediately make you feel like you have stepped back in time and are partaking in a taste of Japanese history. The omuraisu is some of the best we've had. Good food and history equals a definite win!

POCKET TIP

Make sure you get an ice-cream from Long Softcream (2-11-9 Nishishinsaibashi, Chuo-ku) – makers of the allest soft serve in the world, a photo moment if ever there was one.

10 WESTWOOD BAKERS

1-16-9 Minamihorie, Nishi-ku
6538 0022
Mon–Sun 9am–7pm
Yotsubashi station, exit 5
[MAP p. 156 B2]

Westwood say 'we baked our bread for your little happiness', which seems to sum up this simple, small bakery that happily deals in western-style breakfasts and baking for the locals. In a city that sleeps in when it comes to cafes (most open at 11am or later), its 9am opening time makes for a great spot to grab breakfast. Freshly baked bread, donuts (try the coconut) and muffins or a more extensive breakfast of eggs or granola give you plenty of options. Great coffee and sweet things make it the perfect stop later in the day as well, although any of the baked goods will have definitely sold out by then.

POCKET TIP

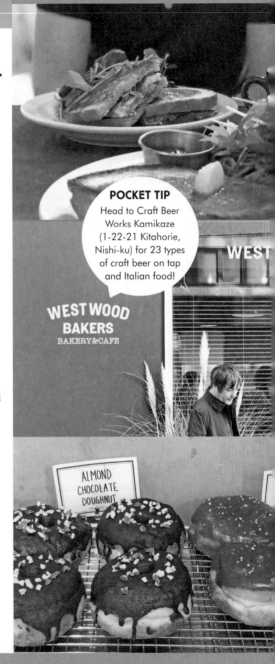

Head to Craft Beer Works Kamikaze (1-22-21 Kitahorie, Nishi-ku) for 23 types of craft beer on tap and Italian food!

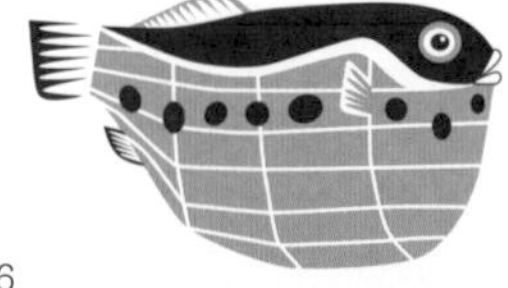

POCKET TIP

Shizen Bar Paprika Shokudo (1-9-9 Nishi-ku, Shinmachi) nearby serves vegan shokudo (casual dining).

11 YAOYA-TO GOHAN SHIMIZU

1-4-14 Kitahorie, Nishi-ku
6532 3381
Mon–Sun 11am–11pm
Yotsubashi station or Shinsaibashi station, exit 5
[MAP p. 158 B2]

Small, colourful noren curtains with vegetable designs are the first sign that you are about to indulge in an organic, healthy and rustic lunch at rowdy and friendly Yaoya. The theme continues inside with pictures of farmers and honest country folk with warming smiles plucking robust looking vegetables from the soil. A frenetic open kitchen looks over a room with fridges stocked with large daikon, small tatami booths for a cosy lunch and large communal tables for getting amongst it. You can choose from a range of rustic and healthy teishoku (small dish) lunch-sets, featuring a meat, fish or vegetarian choice, and a range of small satellite bowls, including pickles, miso, rice and salad. We love the lightly stewed sesame eggplant. Sets include the Prevention Plate, Nourishing Plate, Athlete's Plate, Recovery Plate or Energy Plate – all calorie counted and perfectly balanced. You'll walk out feeling healthy and happy.

12 KOGARYU TAKOYAKI

2-18-4 Shinmachi, Nishi-ku
6211 0519
Mon–Sun 10.30am–8.30pm
Yotsubashi station, exit 5
[MAP p. 158 C3]

On the edge of Triangle Park (*see* p. 77) stands a 30-year-old takoyaki (battered and fried octopus ball) institution. Shambolic and colourful, it's the perfect hole-in-the-wall street food stop. It's famous for a delicious takoyaki and a simple but inspired criss-cross application of mayonnaise, similar to the way it's put on okonomiyaki (Japanese pancake omelette). Takoyaki travel in packs so you'll need to order at least six; one is never enough anyway. If you are a fan of the gooey octopus ball, or you like to people-watch the vibrant, bustling locals, rehearsing comedians and Sunday strollers, this is a must stop on your culinary list.

POCKET TIP

You can find other Kogaryu stands dotted around Osaka. There's a handy one in the Bay Area near Universal Studios and the aquarium.

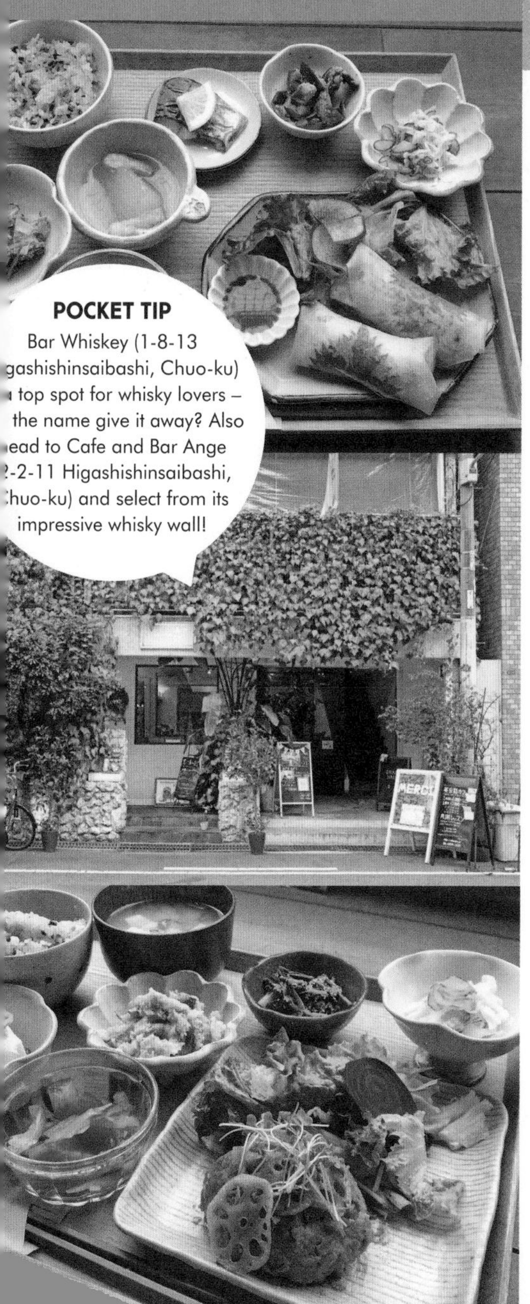

POCKET TIP

Bar Whiskey (1-8-13 gashishinsaibashi, Chuo-ku) top spot for whisky lovers – the name give it away? Also ead to Cafe and Bar Ange -2-11 Higashishinsaibashi, huo-ku) and select from its impressive whisky wall!

13 CAFÉ ORI ORI

2nd floor Pan bldg, 1-9-14
Kitahorie, Nishi-ku
6575 9266
Mon–Sat 11am–4pm, Sat
11am–5pm
Yotsubashi station, exit 4
[MAP p. 158 A1]

Hidden behind a wall of greenery and cascading ivy you'll find your own secret garden of sorts, a quiet, out-of-the-way small shokudo (casual dining) cafe. Home-style food is served, unfussy and delicious – like the kind Mom used to make if you grew up in Japan (the rest of us can certainly feel the comforting hug). Lunch-sets contain delicious staples, wholesome vegetables, pimped-up rice, tasty salads and other small dishes of healthy, hearty food, including shiso leaf rice paper dipping rolls, potato salads, root vegetable patties and miso soup. The interior is darling: under 20 seats with wooden cafeteria tables, a wooden bar, mismatched and repurposed school chairs and low-hanging industrial lighting. There are plenty of delicious desserts and drinks on offer so refuel with afternoon tea. Vegetarians note: like most of Japan there is a set lunch, which might contain a meat dish (maybe swap a plate with your date), but with around eight dishes on your tray, you'll still leave full and satisfied.

OSAKA CASTLE AREA

Osaka has history and heart but sometimes it gets lost in the mayhem, superstructures, family fun destinations, street hawkers, over-the-top shopping malls and mad, mad crush of locals and visitors. Osaka Castle's (*see* p. 92) grounds are a reminder that the city has an incredible historical monument quietly watching over it. These are the hallowed grounds of Naniwa, the Osaka of old. The castle is a major tourist destination but the vast scope of the grounds keeps large crowds at bay. It's a pivotal point – the surrounding area is a bit of a secret – with plenty to explore, most people travel here for the castle but they don't go any further.

Spiralling out in concentric circles from the castle are historical buildings, shrines, gardens, galleries and museums, all crowned by bridges that straddle the northern Daini Neya and Neya rivers. If you're hungry after exploring the castle, you can pop into one of the many popular ramen and noodle shops to the south. Don't miss chic design store Mabataki (*see* p. 94) or the illuminating Osaka Museum of History (*see* p. 93).

→ *Osaka Castle*

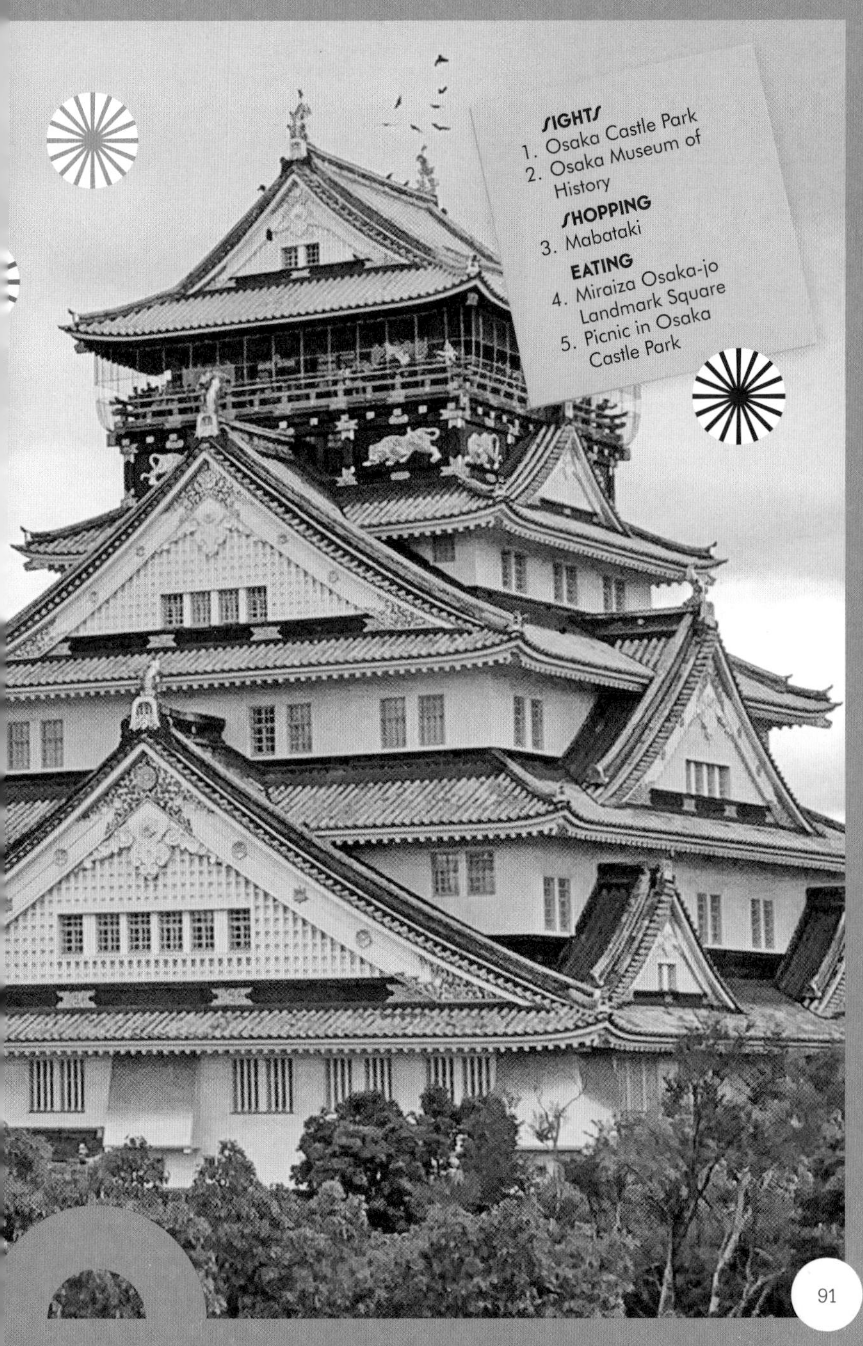
SIGHTS
1. Osaka Castle Park
2. Osaka Museum of History
SHOPPING
3. Mabataki
EATING
4. Miraiza Osaka-jo Landmark Square
5. Picnic in Osaka Castle Park

1 OSAKA CASTLE PARK

1-1 Osakajo, Chuo-ku
6941 3044
Mon–Sun 9am–5pm
Osakajo Koen station, exit 2
[MAP p. 170 B2]

Dating back to 1583, Osaka Castle has been a site of sieges, battles and political intrigue for centuries. The largest castle in Japan at the time of construction, it was rebuilt in 1931 and later refurbished in 1997, a mostly contemporary structure (we're pretty sure the original castle wasn't fitted out with elevators …), but one that still packs a visual punch. Buildings, turrets, gates, stone walls and moats, all from various moments in the castle's history, make for an impressive wander. Inside you'll find artefacts from its extensive history, including armour, scrolls and original architectural features spread out over several floors, which culminate in a wonderful view over the city. The castle itself is a staggering vista and a wonderful photo opportunity from various angles around the grounds. Inside the castle grounds, **Nishinomaru Garden** has over 300 cherry trees and is one of Osaka's most popular spots for sakura (cherry blossom) viewing and picnics in April.

2 OSAKA MUSEUM OF HISTORY

4-1-32 Otemae, Chuo-ku
6946 5728
Wed–Mon 9.30am–5pm
Tanimachi Yonchome station, exit 2 & 9
[MAP p. 170 A3]

History buffs should make a beeline to the south-west corner of the castle grounds to the Osaka Museum of History. Head to the tenth floor, from where you can enjoy excellent views of the castle, and then slowly make your way down through the building, while also moving forward in time. The museum starts with Osaka's beginnings in the mid-7th century to the late-8th century, when **Naniwa-no-miya Palace** (partially recreated on this floor) was the seat of government. The palace ruins, unearthed in 1953, can be seen below from the large windows. Subsequent floors then track Osaka's development from a trading port in the middle ages through to modernity, until arriving at the 20th century, with various brightly coloured life-sized panoramas depicting street scenes, buildings and modern life. The recreated **Kabuki Theatre** is a treat. Lower floors feature revolving exhibitions – don't miss the recreation of a 5th century **Hoenzaka Warehouse** outside the building.

POCKET TIP

Adjacent to the Osaka Museum of History is the impressive NHK Osaka Hall Television Studio, where visitors can tour an array of facilities.

3 MABATAKI

2-26-18 Nakamichi,
Higashinari-ku
Mon–Sun 10am–7pm (closed every second Wed)
Morinomiya station, exit 5
[MAP p. 171 C3]

Mabataki means eye blink, an action we make every day. The chic but down-to-earth designer store offers goods that are special, but that they would like you to use in a casual and natural way – almost as if blinking, hence the name. Mabataki design and make their clothes in-store using Japanese cotton. The men's and women's clothing is relaxed, yet stylish – and made to feel like something you would pick out of your wardrobe to wear daily – a go-to T-shirt, trousers or a simple dress. You could buy a timeless capsule wardrobe here that would get better with age. We love their faded indigo blue cotton bags that are simply constructed, elegant and breezy. Mabataki also design their own tableware and have pieces made by artisans in Kyoto. Expect enamelware, ceramics, kitchenalia and macramé pot plant holders among their range.

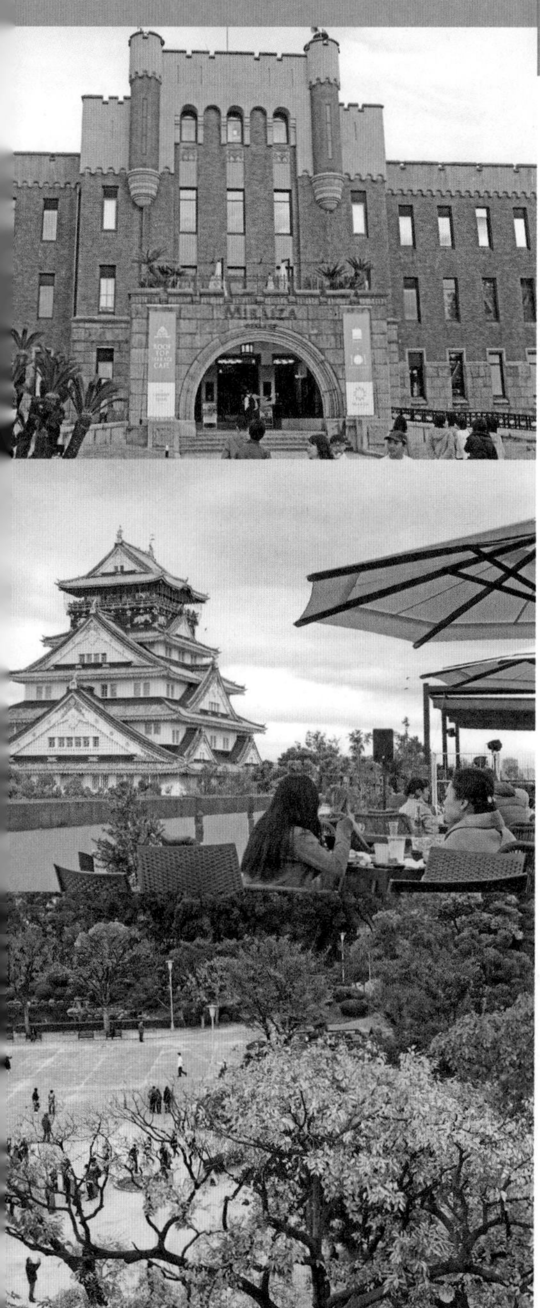

4 MIRAIZA OSAKA-JO LANDMARK SQUARE

Chuo-ku
66941 7100
Mon–Sun 11am–3pm, 5–10pm
Osakajo Koen station, exit 2
[MAP p. 170 C2]

Positioned in the actual grounds of Osaka Castle (*see* p. 92), in view of the castle tower, is a new shopping and food destination. It was constructed within the austere 86-year-old former Japanese Imperial Army Military Barracks, with Romanesque architecture in the front hall and a beautiful staircase leading up to stained-glass windows and Art Deco hanging lights. Head up to the second and third floors, collectively known as **Landmark Square**, and splash a bit of cash to dine at **Raspberry**. Check out their **Moon Bar**, which was designed with the original creator of Osaka Castle, Toyotomi Hideyoshi, in mind. Your main goal though, should be **Blue Birds** on the rooftop terrace; there is an entrance fee that covers one drink, but mostly it's a great place to relax, while taking in full views of the castle – and it's particularly romantic at night.

5 PICNIC IN OSAKA CASTLE PARK

Osakajo Koen station, exit 2
[MAP p. 170 B2]

Osaka Castle (*see* p. 92) is a premium tourist destination, but it can be difficult to find good food in between castle viewings. Once the metaphorical drawbridge has been raised, ninja shopping and general roaming for photo opportunities becomes a priority. We recommend a picnic lunch in the castle grounds. You'll avoid all the over-priced and underwhelming food offerings, keep away from the crowds, if the season is right, and languish under the autumn leaves or sakura (cherry blossoms). Curate your own packed lunch before you go, from one of the many simple eateries in the surrounding precinct or visit **Lawson Station** on the south-east side of the grounds (near the taxi rank), to stock up on delicious onigiri, salads, oden, nuts, fresh edamame, crackers and seasonal treats. There is also a delicious range of sweet things, including ice-creams, mochi and vegan desserts. Yogurts, soy drinks, alcohol and hot canned coffee round off the array of picnic surprises, so stock up before you attempt to breach the castle.

黄金からあげ ¥500　紅ずわい入りにぎり天 ¥500
にぎり天
一串 ¥500（税込）
お酒
大阪城で
かんぱ
500Yen
500Yen

TENMA

Take your time and stroll around Tenma, where you'll connect with an intimate piece of Osaka. The name Tenma (Temma) is drawn from one of the area's major attractions, Osaka Tenmangu Shrine (*see* p. 100). However, Tenma is more than just the shrine – it has carved out a niche as a place to get away from the crowds, to experience some exceptional food, local history and secret indie stores like Second Banana (*see* p. 106) and Yonagadou (*see* p. 105), all hidden among the lesser trodden streets. Central hub Tenjinbashi-suji Shopping Street (*see* p. 102) is a giant covered arcade, one of Japan's longest, crammed with discount shops, retro stores and the occasional standout restaurant. Harukoma Honten Sushi (*see* p. 107) is unmissable for lovers of an authentic sushi experience.

In Ura-Tenma, north of Tenma station, you'll find a clutch of bars and diners, with some premium eating and drinking that takes on an almost magical presence at night. Small alleys crammed with izakaya (pubs with small-plate food), hole-in-the-wall eateries and standing bars buzz with locals and residents sampling Osaka street food and simple international food. Nearby Chochin-dori is a retro maze of old-school bars and eateries.

→ *Visitors at the Osaka Tenmangu Shrine*

SIGHTS
1. Osaka Tenmangu Shrine
2. Osaka Museum of Housing and Living
SHOPPING
3. Tenjinbashi-suji Shopping Street
4. Teoriya
EATING & DRINKING
5. Ura-Tenma & Chochin-dori
6. Yonagadou
7. Second Banana
8. Harukoma Honten Sushi

1 OSAKA TENMANGU SHRINE

2-1-8 Tenjinbashi, Kita-ku
Mon–Sun 9am-5pm
Osaka Temmangu station, exit 7
[MAP p. 169 B2]

If you feel smarter when you enter Osaka Tenmangu Shrine, it's because the 10th-century Shinto shrine is dedicated to the god of scholarship, Sugawara no Michizane. Say a quick prayer here for success in upcoming studies, exams or the pub trivia quiz. As with many millennium-old shrines, the original buildings were reduced to ashes by fire, the main hall and gate date to 1845. You might find the large grounds surprising, considering Tenmangu's big city location. Also surprising is the lack of tourist traffic. Standout points are tori gates leading to small altars; the colourful zodiac emblem and shimenawa (enclosing rope) above the impressive daimon gate; and the rows of blue and white lanterns offset against the ornate gold and dark woods of the main shrine. Search out three historic buildings in the grounds: Kaguraden, Shushuden and Umebana for bonsai exhibitions, plum blossoms and the beautiful katsuyama water garden.

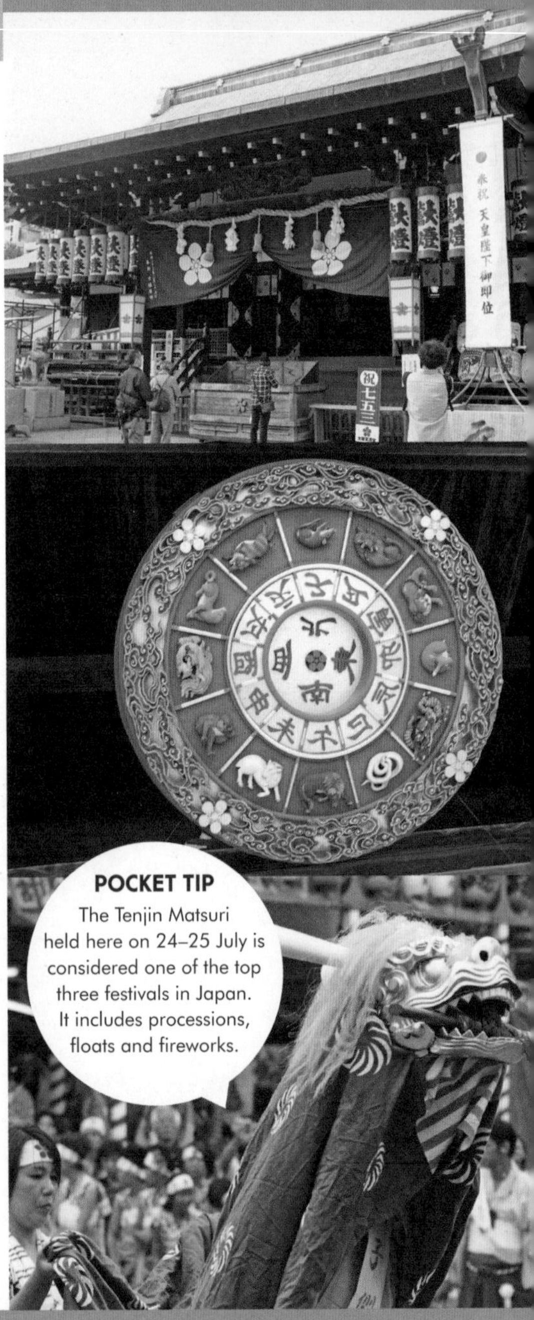

POCKET TIP

The Tenjin Matsuri held here on 24–25 July is considered one of the top three festivals in Japan. It includes processions, floats and fireworks.

POCKET TIP

Feeling nostalgic for old-school cash in the cashless economy? Visit the Osaka Mint Bureau (1-1-79 Tenma, Kita-ku) and peruse its extensive collection of coins or admire over 300 cherry blossoms in the garden (when in season).

2 OSAKA MUSEUM OF HOUSING AND LIVING

6-4-20 Tenjinbashisuji, Kita-ku
Mon–Sun 10am–4.30pm
Tenjimbashisujirokuchome station, exit 3
[MAP p. 168 A1]

At the northern end of Tenjinbashi-suji, you'll find the Osaka Museum of Housing and Living. Sounds thrilling? Actually, it is. This museum recreates full-sized houses and streets from many of the classic eras of Japanese architecture in Osaka – and it does it so well. Stroll the Edo-era (1603–1868) streets, where a whole section of the city is reborn in the building (it even features a bathhouse). You can hire a kimono and really feel like you are living a part of history, as you shop in various themed stores for sweets or souvenirs (prices don't reflect the eras – allow for inflation). Other eras have similar standout recreations and exhibits, including Meiji (1868–1912), Taisho (1912–26) and Showa (1926–89). It's great fun for kids and adults alike, and a chance to literally place yourself within the history of Osaka.

3 TENJINBASHI-SUJI SHOPPING STREET

Tenjinbashi, Kita-ku
Hours vary
Ogimachi, Tenjimbashisujirokuchome, Minamimorimachi, Temma & Osaka–Temmangu stations
[MAP p. 168 A3]

Tenjinbashi-suji is one of Japan's longest covered shopping arcades, seven blocks of quaint vintage shopping punctuated by ¥100 shops, discount chemists, pachinko parlours and the odd Japanese chain cafe. Its roots stretch back to around 1653, when it began as a merchant street, with many fresh produce stores picking up business from pilgrims as they walked towards Osaka Tenmangu Shrine (*see* p. 100). Many of the 600 plus stores are decades old, and the distinct lack of international brands and high-end fashion gives the street a timeless charm. There is a mix of old-timers whiling away the hours in majong parlours, bookstores with teetering piles of tomes rich with the smell of their faded pages and Mom and Pop eateries with wizened, time-worn workers. A plethora of street eat stalls mean you can eat as you walk, or stop into cheap sushi and ramen restaurants along the way. It's a nostalgic wander and a chance to connect with Osaka's past.

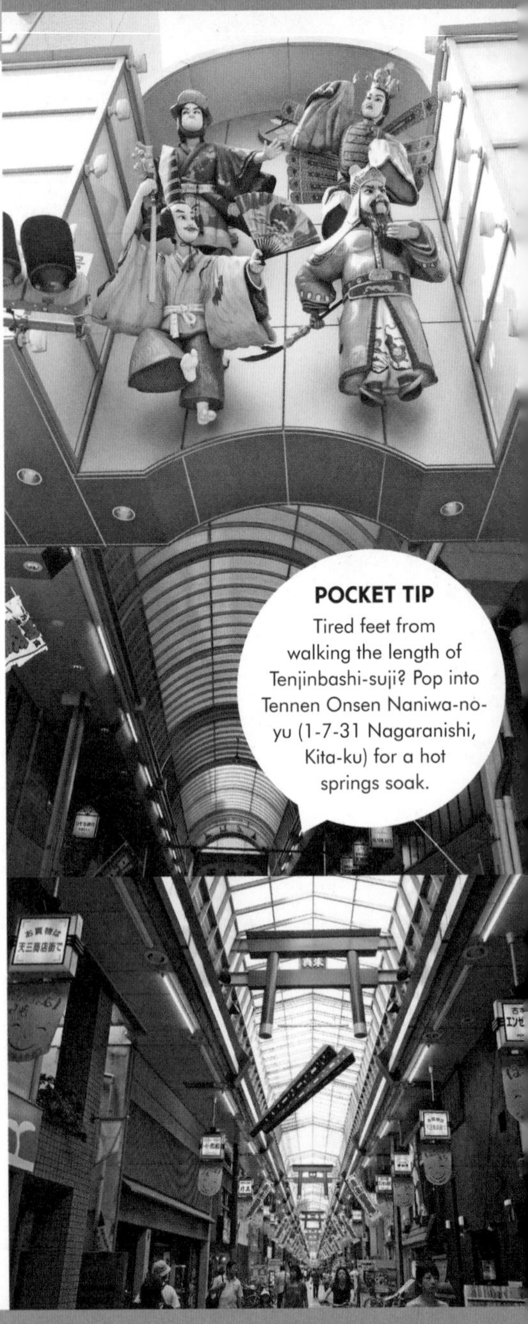

POCKET TIP

Tired feet from walking the length of Tenjinbashi-suji? Pop into Tennen Onsen Naniwa-no-yu (1-7-31 Nagaranishi, Kita-ku) for a hot springs soak.

POCKET TIP
RJ Café (3-2-1 Tenma, Kita-ku) do a coffee that comes in an edible biscuit cup – delicious AND eco-friendly.

4 TEORIYA

2-5-34 Tenjinbashi, Kita-ku
www.teoriya.net
Mon–Fri 10am–6pm
Osaka–Temmangu station, exit 8
[MAP p. 169 B1]

People go to Japan in search of many things and for crafters, a good yarn is one of them. Okay, we're sure this shop tells a good story, but we're referring to wool, silk, cotton and linen. Walls of it, in fact, laid out in brightly coloured rows of classic-style yarn twists, just waiting for someone nimble with knitting needles to turn a skein into a skivvy or a jumbuck into a jumper. With over three thousand different types of yarn on offer, you'll easily find what you are looking for. If the shelves of bright colours inspire you to get creative, they also run classes. The store looks great from the outside: a warm wooden frontage with looms and knitting wheels visible through the windows and a row of fluffy black sheep walking along the roof of the building. They have an online store if you get home and find that you are a few stitches short of a row.

5 URA-TENMA & CHOCHIN DORI

[MAP p. 168 C4]

As night falls, head to the north exit of Tenma station to find the area magically transformed into a neon-lit wonderland of enticing alleys, luminous bars and spirited hole-in-the-wall eateries. Izakayas (pubs with small-plate food), soba noodle joints, sushi, yakiniku (grilled meat), yakitori and standing bars make the area one of Osaka's must-hit nighttime spots. Nearby Chochin-dori is a yokocho (rabbit warren) of drinking alleys, with a central arcade strewn with 700 chochin lanterns (bamboo folding lanterns often found outside izakaya). **Kobachiya Bar** specialises in a fast-growing trend of choinomi and choitabe (small drinks and small bites), which include unmissable black wagyu and sea urchin. **Orb** masters the cheeky crustacean, excelling in shrimp and lobster dishes. **Yoidore Kujira** is a beautiful space specialising in tempura, smoked food and wine. For the adventurous, **Nikuzushi** swaps out fish for meat to create a new kind of sushi. Stop off for a drink at **Beer Belly Tenma** where the bar is 12 metres (39 feet) long and the draught beer is served up with delicious snacks.

POCKET TIP

Pulala Tenma (3-3-1 Ikedacho, Kita-ku) is a lively traditional indoor fo market featuring stalls wi fresh produce and plent of take-away snacks.

6 YONAGADOU

Tatsuta Bldg, 2F, 3-4-5 Tenma, Kita-ku
Thurs–Tues 12pm–7pm
Tenmabashi station, exit 2
[MAP p. 169 C3]

The Tatsuta Building is a secret pocket of Osaka, a faceless building that holds a handful of Osaka's most interesting destinations. Climb the stairs to visit crafter and maker Tatsuko-san's secret, super-cute zakka (miscellaneous everyday items) store on the second floor of the building. Yonagadou sells kokeshi dolls, lucky cats, reproduction paper, vintage tableware and repurposed furniture. The curation here is an interesting mix of ephemera, so if you are looking for a Japanese take on an indie aesthetic, then this is the place to come. They also have a great range of irresistible small items, like kawaii toys and stationery and handkerchiefs (or cloth wrapping). Michelle loves their printed fabric designs, her favourite way to eco wrap presents and omiyage (regional souvenirs). To the side of the store is a little gallery showcasing indie creations from local and international artists.

POCKET TIP

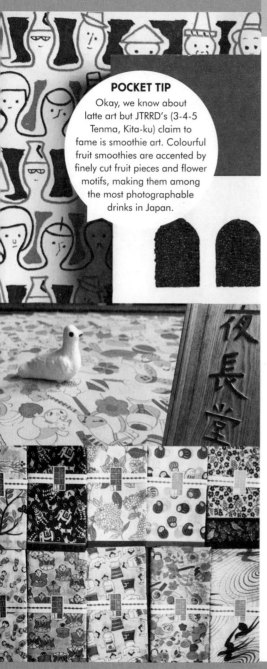

Okay, we know about latte art but JTRRD's (3-4-5 Tenma, Kita-ku) claim to fame is smoothie art. Colourful fruit smoothies are accented by finely cut fruit pieces and flower motifs, making them among the most photographable drinks in Japan.

7 SECOND BANANA

3-4-22 Tenma, Kita-ku
6242 0877
Mon–Sun 11am–6pm
Osaka–Temmangu station, exit 7
[MAP p. 169 C4]

If you like to have lunch and drink coffee while sitting under a giant flying Astro Boy, or watched over by the HMV dog, then this is the place for you. Second Banana is an antique shop crammed with a disparate mix of engaging paraphernalia, stuffed bookshelves, fire-king ceramics, oil drums and garage tools. The walls feature name-related bits and bobs, like a cover of The Velvet Underground's classic album with the Warhol Banana, plus dartboards, clocks, Shell oil signs and vintage posters. The cafe serves simple curries and drip-filter or plunger coffee underneath low hanging lights and voluminous hanging pot plants.

POCKET TIP

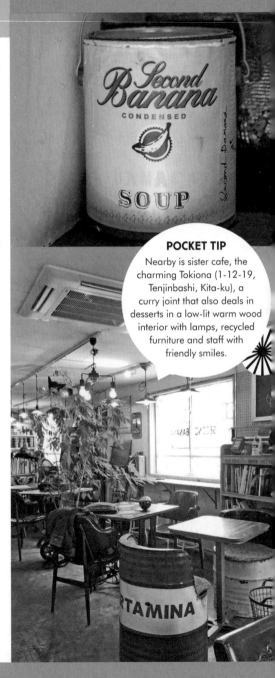

Nearby is sister cafe, the charming Tokiona (1-12-19, Tenjinbashi, Kita-ku), a curry joint that also deals in desserts in a low-lit warm wood interior with lamps, recycled furniture and staff with friendly smiles.

8 HARUKOMA HONTEN SUSHI

5-5-2 Tenjinbashi, Kita-ku
6351 4319
Wed–Mon 11am–10pm
Tenjimbashisuji station, exit 12
[MAP p. 168 B3]

Forget what you know about the delicate art of thinly sliced and beautifully arranged sushi. Harukoma Honten *is* in Osaka and as a result, subtlety goes out the window and sushi becomes a chunkier, less precious affair. This is Osaka going large with portions of sushi that go for a budget-friendly price-point but doesn't sacrifice quality. Naturally the joint is rowdy, joyous and crammed with beer-fuelled locals. Join the queue, duck under the noren curtain and order up sushi platters that can barely fit onto the plates (actually very stylish black slate platters – a nice touch), and sushi rolls that can barely contain their fillings. The menu also includes miso bowls piled high with clams, thick-set sashimi and various seafood platters of fish: known and unknown. Spacious, friendly and fun, it's an authentic sushi stop – and it's near the south end of Tenjinbashisuji, making it the perfect place to take a break between shopping and heading to the drinking holes around Tenma station.

SHINSEKAI & TENNOJI

Set up as the perfect modern Japanese town for the 1970 World Fair, Shinsekai was long thought of as an out-of-date, even dangerous, area. Its retro charm is now a destination, a crazy pop-colour landscape of in-your-face signs and tempting street food stalls. The loose nature of Shinsekai – the raucous crowds, the 'out for fun' attitude, the mad hues of the street signs, boisterous bellow of the street hawkers and tourists tripping over other tourists trying to get that perfectly angled shot – make it a one-of-a-kind experience. The colourful, giant pufferfish flapping in the breeze with the panoramic view of the Tsutenkaku Tower (*see* p. 110) behind it, is a vista like no other. If you're hungry, this is the town of cheap eats, especially kushikatsu (fried food on skewers), takoyaki (battered octopus dumplings) and ramen. Charming covered arcades with longstanding Mom and Pop stores tendril off from the main street.

Further south in Tennoji, the traditional enclave of Shitennoji Temple (*see* p. 111) is perfect for a stroll in a more peaceful part of Osaka. The impish character you'll see everywhere in this precinct is Billiken, the area's good luck mascot.

→ *Kushikatsu Takoyaki Ajinodaimaru*

SIGHTS

1. Tsutenkaku Tower
2. Shitennoji Temple
3. Spa World
4. Love Hotels

SHOPPING

5. Tower Knives

EATING & DRINKING

6. Uesugi Liquor Store drink machines
7. Kushikatsu street food
8. Zuboraya Shinsekai
9. Rokusen

1 TSUTENKAKU TOWER

1-18-6 Ebisuhigashi, Naniwa-ku
6641 9555
Mon–Sun 9am–9pm
Ebisuchu station, exit 3
[MAP p. 174 B2]

The 'Eiffel Tower' of Osaka was originally built in 1912, stunning the population with its frightening 64 metre (210 feet) height. Built to mimic both the Eiffel Tower and the Arc de Triomphe (an arch forms the base of the tower), it was the tallest man-made structure in Asia at the time, gaining status as the 'symbol of Osaka'. Fire damaged it beyond repair in 1943 and its skeleton of steel was disassembled to provide precious materials for the war effort. In 1956 a new tower rose like a phoenix from the ashes. At 103 metres (337 feet) tall it eclipsed the original (designer Tachu Naito also designed Tokyo Tower). The tower is a faded marvel, an old-world glimpse into Shinsekai's past. Inside, you'll find souvenir shops but you should take the elevator up to two observation decks on the fourth and fifth floors, both with excellent views of the surrounding neon-lit streetscapes and the lush expanse of Tennoji Park.

POCKET TIP

At 300 metres (984 feet) tall, Abeno Harukas is the tallest building in Japan and has a spectacular view from Harukas 300 on floors 58–60.

POCKET TIP
Isshinji Temple dates back to the 12th century and features a very contemporary gate and statue approach, designed by the current head priest.

2 SHITENNOJI TEMPLE

1-11-18 Shitennoji, Tennoji-ku
6771 0066
Mon–Sun 8am–4pm
Shitennoji-Mae Yuhigaoka station, exit 3
[MAP p. 175 B3]

Considered the oldest Buddhist temple in Japan, Shitennoji was founded by Prince Shotoku Taishi in 593. The Shitenno are the four heavenly kings of Buddhist teaching who watch over the world, protecting it from evil. Many rebuilds over the years have remained faithful to the original structures. Standout sights include the **Chushin Garan**, which features a Kondo or main hall (the Prince is cannonised here); a unique and ornate five storey **pagoda**; a treasure house featuring many of the temple's original valuables; the **Benzaiten Shrine**, dedicated to the river goddess and 'all things that flow'; and the **Gokurakujodo Garden** (Buddhist Paradise), with its thousands of cherry trees. On the 21st and 22nd of each month the temple features the popular **Shitennoji flea market**, which runs from 8am to 6pm. Free to enter, you'll find over 300 stalls selling vintage clothes, fabric, ceramics and retro paraphernalia, plus plenty of food stalls.

3 SPA WORLD

3-4-24 Ebisuhigashi, Naniwa-ku
Mon–Sun open 24 hrs
Dobutsuen-Mae station, exit 5
[MAP p. 174 B3]

This is how Osaka does a super sento (large communal bath house): big, bold and over the top. The range of baths and experiences here turn the revered Japanese onsen (hot springs bath) into a bit of a theme park, but you'll be too relaxed to notice. Spa World is where Doctor Who goes when he needs to bathe and relax after saving the universe. It's a country hopping, time zone-changing world of water where you can relax in Rome, gleam in Greece, absorb in Asia and bathe in Bali (mythological explorers among you will love the 'Atlantis' bath). An extensive sauna section takes you through Turkish steam baths and Finland wood saunas, salt saunas, mud spas and, of course, there is massage, rest rooms and plenty of eating and drinking opportunities. Spa World rotates areas monthly for each gender, and look online to see if you are getting the world experience or the Asian experience. Switch off and soak, just don't be surprised if you find yourself adrift in time and space.

4 LOVE HOTELS

The appropriately named Hotel Love, which opened in 1968, inspired the name 'Love Hotel' and although it is no more, its satin-sheeted memory lives on in the hearts and minds (and possibly the children) of an older generation in Osaka. Of course Osaka had to be the birthplace (that's what can happen if you don't use protection) of the love hotel – short stay, pay-by-the-hour, 'no tell' hotels, often themed and mostly used for romantic trysts, afternoon delights or behind-closed-doors capers of one kind or another. Between Tennoji and Sennichimae-suji you'll find many of Osaka's Love Hotels, and time hasn't made them any less over-the-top. **Hotel Public Jam** includes a carnival themed room complete with carousel; **Hotel Love** (a different one) has an obsessive attention to wallpaper and flowers); and **Hotel Ikutama Love** lays on the romance with jacuzzis, massage chairs, flowers and champagne. The best way to reach them is to find Tanimachikyuchome station, exit N°3 and follow Tanimachi-suji.

5 TOWER KNIVES

1-4-7 Ebisuhigashi, Naniwa-ku
4301 7860
Mon–Sun 10am–6pm
Ebisuchu station, exit 3
[MAP p. 174 B2]

One of Osaka's best knife shops can be found just a little to the side of Tsutenkaku Tower (hence the name, *see* p. 110). Just head towards the zoo and before long you'll find the understated frontage with the green canopy. Knife fanatics will find a sharp (sorry) selection of some of Japan's best blades among the extensive range, all crafted in Japan and many coming from the nearby famous knife town of Sakai (*see* p. 126). If you want to get schooled in Japanese knife life, Tower will gladly demonstrate how knives are made, how to use them, how to sharpen them, grades of steel, the best knives for selected tasks and more. With several expats working there, English conversations are easy. Left-handers rejoice, you can get a knife here (it sounds odd, but the blade of a special knife is on one side so it becomes an issue for left-handers). They will even personalise your knife by engraving your name. Bring your passport, as Tower give tax-free refunds on purchases. And best not to pack in your hand luggage.

6 UESUGI LIQUOR STORE DRINK MACHINES

3-1-17 Ebisuhigashi Naniwa-ku
Mon–Sun 24 hrs
Dobutsuen-Mae station, exit 5
[MAP p. 174 B3]

Japan's classic booze vending machines used to be everywhere – now it's just a select few places that have them and Shinsekai was always going to be one. At the side of a chemist, down a conspicuous laneway, next to an old timers' cafe, butted up against a retro green '70s tiled wall – what better way to have a quiet pick-me-up while navigating the family filled streets. Hang on, I'll just get some soda for the kids from a vending machine … yeah right. An added bonus is that the machines are older now and in some cases have existed since last century, so you'll get a range of retro plum wine shots with the kind of packaging you'd be hunting for at a vintage market. There are also beer cans of all sizes and makers, and ever-popular one-cup sake, all being shiftily perused by many of the Shinsekai locals and regulars … and you.

7 KUSHIKATSU STREET FOOD

Almost every second place in Shinsekai is a kushikatsu shop or stand and that's no exaggeration. Kushikatsu is fried meat or vegetables on skewers, similar to yakitori but with the added kick of a deep-fried breadcrumb crust. It's fast, delicious and the perfect accompaniment to beer – it can soak up anything. Kushikatsu fillings include seafood (fish, oysters, scallops and prawns), meat (pork, beef, minced chicken, quail eggs and various giblets and gizzards), a variety of vegetables and even cheese. Some establishments will offer some culinary challenges, like scorpion, grasshopper, kangaroo or horse. You can order as many as you like and it's a cheap feed. **Kushikatsu Daruma Tsutenkaku** has several eateries in the area, which usually have long queues. Also try **Kushikatsu Murafuji** and **Maru**.

POCKET TIP

Street food is king in Shinsekai – from takoyaki (battered octopus dumplings) to yakitori (grilled meat on skewers), taiyaki (sea bream shaped sweet pastry with filling) and ice-cream – but above all kushikatsu reigns supreme.

8 ZUBORAYA SHINSEKAI

2-5-5 Ebisuhigashi, Naniwa-ku
6633 5529
Mon–Sun 11am–11pm
Dobutsuen station, exit 5
[MAP p. 174 B2]

The famous fat fugu (pufferfish) sign at the front of this restaurant is here for a reason – it's a fugu restaurant. Fugu, a Japanese delicacy, has been spoken of in hushed tones for a while – one slip of the knife by an amateur could puncture the poison sac and means certain death (and not only for the fish: 176 people died from eating fugu in 1958, and between 1996 and 2003 there were 44 deaths by fugu reported). Thus, the preparation of pufferfish is carefully regulated in Japan, you can't use half measures. Once the deadly parts are cut away, you can enjoy fugu as sashimi, grilled or in a chirinabe hot-pot. This famed Osaka restaurant is stunningly visual and a perfect photo opportunity, but it also gives the culinary adventurer a chance to taste the revered fish. It can be expensive to dice with death, so check prices beforehand. Zuboraya serves traditional and simple fugu dishes.

POCKET TIP

Janjan Yokocho is a covered arcade, with funfair-style shooting galleries wedged between long-time eateries and jazz cafes, where old-timers play board games in faded wall kitchenettes and '80s game arcades pop and ping.

9 ROKUSEN

1-17-7 Ebisuhigashi, Naniwa-ku
4301 7860
Mon–Sun 11am–10pm
Ebisucho station, exit 3
[MAP p. 174 B1]

Rokusen is an atmospheric seafood eatery that both belies and embodies the rough and tumble theme of Shinsekai, by serving quality, super fresh fish at the right price in a fast-paced environment. It's a retro shokudo-style (home food) eatery, with a wooden counter table where chefs work in full view preparing a la carte sushi and sashimi, all served to you by long-term workers who flit about frenetically. Order with the tablet, which has an English menu available – make sure to order one kind of fish that you've never tried before. Wash it down with a beer or two to loosen up, ready to head back out into this manic area full of crazy wonder. The name Rokusen (six thousand yen – around 60 cents) relates to the price it used to be – ¥60 for a piece of sushi! Those were the days. It costs a little more now, but not *that* much more.

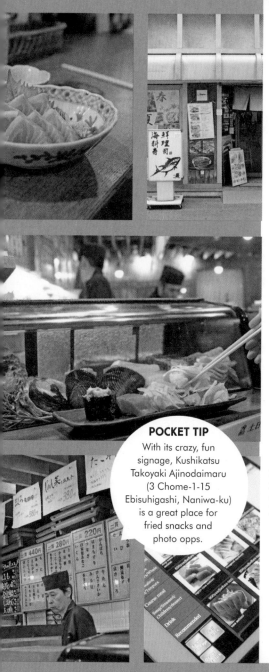

POCKET TIP

With its crazy, fun signage, Kushikatsu Takoyaki Ajinodaimaru (3 Chome-1-15 Ebisuhigashi, Naniwa-ku) is a great place for fried snacks and photo opps.

OSAKA OUTSKIRTS

Osaka has many one-off destinations that exist on the outskirts of the city. Usually a half-day train trip with minimal travel times, our selection will whisk you away from the city centre to quieter retreats. Stepping out of the capital will reward you with experiences that truly embrace Osaka's individual spirit and multi-layered culture.

For bibliophiles, there's the architectural masterpiece of the Shiba Ryotaro Memorial Museum (*see* p. 125) and Hirakata T-Site (*see* p. 128), with its towering wall of books and arresting facade. The town of Sakai (*see* p. 126) makes the best knives in Japan and has a long history of Samurai steel. It also hides one of Japan's ancient secrets, the Mozu Tombs (*see* p. 127). Fans of a tipple will want to embark on two of Japan's best brewery tours, the Suntory Yamazaki Distillery (*see* p. 122) and Asahi Suita Brewery (*see* p. 123). Escape to nature in beautiful Minoo Park (*see* p. 124) or ride the Hankyu Kyo-train Garaku (*see* p. 121), an enchanting weekend ride between Osaka and Kyoto that brings back the spirit of old Japan. The following pages sketch out these adventures and more, so make sure to add some to your itinerary.

HANKYU KYO-TRAIN GARAKU

The Hankyu Kyo-train Garaku began operating in March 2019, setting a new standard in experiential train travel. The train interior is essentially a recreation of a Kyoto Machiya (vintage townhouse), with wood panelling and tatami floors. Other highlights onboard include wood block print wallpaper, themed seat upholstery, washi (paper) posters and even a small Zen garden! Each of the six beautiful carriages reflect a seasonal Kyoto theme. So anyone leaving Kyoto can keep Kyoto beauty in their heart – and anyone leaving Osaka can glimpse some of the serenity they are about to find. Outside carriages are emblazoned with intricate Japanese fans, maple leaves and seasonal motifs. The interior references famous Kyoto sights, festivals, food and castles. The train fare is inexpensive – think local prices under ¥500 for one way. The train runs every two hours from 9.32am to 3.32pm (weekends only). Arrive early and queue for the carriage of your choice.

From Osaka–Umeda station on the Hankyu line to Kyoto–Kawaramachi station (45 min).

SUNTORY YAMAZAKI DISTILLERY

5-2-1 Yamazaki, Shimamoto-cho
75 962 1423
www.suntory.com/factory/yamazaki
Mon–Sun 9.30am–5pm

Surrounded by lush vegetation at the foot of Mount Tennozan, the Suntory Yamazaki Distillery holds the history of Japanese whisky in its veins. Japan's first, it was started in 1923 by Shinjiro Torii and Masataka Taketsuru who wanted to perfect distillation. Suntory whisky is now famous the world-over, winning the gold medal for its 12-year single-malt whisky in 2003 and beating the Scottish at their own game to become world leaders in 2017. Take the 80-minute-long tour or wander around at your own leisure to see the rows and rows of wooden vats, eye-popping distillation room and a 'whisky library', featuring thousands of different varieties. For whisky obsessives, you can do tastings of some of the great vintages for a fraction of the price you would pay in a bar. And don't forget to exit via the gift shop! Make sure you reserve online. You must be at least 20 years old to visit.

From Osaka–Umeda station on the JR Tokaido line to Yamazaki station (about 26 min).

POCKET TIP

Explore the Asahi area for some great finds, including Bird Coffee (4-1-16 Midori, Tsurumi-ku) and Truck Furniture (6-8-48 Shinmori, Asahi-ku).

ASAHI SUITA BREWERY & BEER FACTORY TOUR

1-45 Nishinoshocho, Suita
6388 1943
Mon–Sun 9.30am–3pm

Without being 'super-dry' about it, there are Asahi Beer factory tours all over Japan – but the Asahi Suita Brewery was the first and has a 110-year-history of beer production. It's the beer-o-philes go-to when it comes to drinking in all you can about the process of beer making. The tour is the perfect mid-pint – I mean mid-point – between an instructive museum on beer making, outlining a deep history of the facility, and Willy Wonka's Beer Factory: think colourful chequered floors, and an intricate main hall with looming vats and spaghetti-like pipes. For us, the standout is the colourful wall of beer cans and the graphics for different beer types from the past century. For most people however, the standout is probably the twenty minutes' 'tasting time' at the end. The foamy head on top of the beer is that the factory tour is free – and so is the tasting! You'll walk out tipsy with excitement (or beer) and with a newfound appreciation for one of Japan's best beers, offset only by tomorrow's hangover.

From Osaka–Umeda station on the JR Kyoto line to Suita station (9 min).

MINOO PARK

Minookoen, Minoo
72 723 1885
Fri–Wed 10am–4pm

The Hankyu Railway will transport you to the lush valleys and glades of Minoo Park (officially called Meiji no Mori Minoō Kokutei Kōen). It's a beautiful natural enclave, particularly in autumn, when the trees brush the landscape with luminous red and gold girding the Minoo waterfall. Snap pictures of your loved one on the beautiful vermillion bridge with the waterfall tumbling behind. Minoo's trails, rivers and waterfalls are a local Osaka secret – a welcome diversion from the big city. Peaceful **Shotengu Saikoji temple** leads to a beautiful walk along the **Takimichi trail**, which features a ryokan, shrines and temples. Budding entomologists should stop off at the **Insect Museum** – the area is crawling with all manner of six-legged species. The butterfly garden will fill your heart with flutters. Aesthetic 7th-century temple **Ryuan-ji** is associated with luck, in fact it is said that the lottery began here.

POCKET TIP

End your day with a soak at Minoo Onsen Spa (with spectacular Osaka city views) to complete a perfect city retreat.

From Osaka–Umeda station on the Hankyu Railway to Minoo station (25 min).

SHIBA RYOTARO MEMORIAL MUSEUM

3-11-18 Shimokosaka,
Higashiosaka city
6726 3860
Tues–Sun 10am–5pm

A mesmerising and inspirational vision, and one of the final words on memorial museums and architecture, Ryotaro Library is simply breathtaking. Shiba Ryotaro was one of Japan's most celebrated writers. Particularly loved are his historical novels, many of which have been made into popular films. In 2001, famed architect Tadao Ando constructed this monumental shrine to the written word, dedicated to Ryotaro. The 11-metre-high (36 feet) walls of books, featuring some 20,000 tomes, are stunning. The striking wall of wooden shelving that girds the main room, traversed by walkways and staircases, is reminiscent of a fantastical European library. Be inspired and set up at a work space to study, read and feel Ryotaro's creative spirit. You can even see a small exhibit of the cosy room where Ryotaro worked later in life.

From Osaka-Umeda station on the loop line to Tsuruhashi station and on the Kintetsu-Nara line to Yaenosato station (30 min).

SAKAI (KNIFE CAPITAL)

A historic Japanese seaport stretching back to medieval times, Sakai stands at the mouth of the Yamato River with Osaka Bay lapping at its heels. One of Japan's most intriguing destinations resides here, the **Mozu Tombs** (*see* p. 127). However, the city's main claim-to-fame is a 600-year-history of forging iron and making Japan's best quality kitchen knives; it was once the primary producer of exquisite samurai swords. The knives pass through the skilled hands of four different makers: blacksmith, grinder, handle-maker and assembler, who make sure blade and handle are perfectly aligned. It is estimated that 90 per cent of professional chefs in Japan use knives from Sakai, a ringing endorsement. You can buy direct from many blacksmiths, or head to famed knife shops, like **Jikko** or **Kawamura**, or in Osaka, check out **Tower Knives** (*see* p. 115) or knife shops in **Sennichimae Doguyasuji Shotengai** (*see* p. 52). A note from Michelle to left-handers: your knife maker will ask if you are left- or right-handed, meaning you can finally get one that is comfortable for you to use.

From Osaka–Namba station on the Nankai Airport Express to Sakai station (10 min).

MOZU TOMBS

3-357-1 Mozu Nishinocho,
Kita-ku, Sakai
6210 9742
Mon–Sun 24 hrs

The Mozu Tombs were built between the 4th and 6th centuries for the kofun (ruling elite). They received a UNESCO World Heritage Listing in June 2019. The tombs themselves are nothing more than markers, memorials, mounds and burial plots in various locations around Sakai. Some command huge areas however and a unique feature of the bigger tombs is that from the air and surrounding highlands, the grounds and moat make the shape of a keyhole. People believe that Emperor Nintoku is buried in the largest of the tombs, called the **Emperor Nintoku Kofun**, which is considered to be one of the largest graves in the world, and is certainly the largest in Japan. **Daisen Park** is a good place to go, as it features many of the area's best tombs and a beautiful **Japanese garden**. Hiking around the area is very popular. A quaint fact: the tombs are all literally right next door to local houses, buildings and office blocks.

From Osaka–Namba station on the Nankai Airport Express to Sakai station (10 min).

HIRAKATA T-SITE

1 2-2 Okahigashicho, Hirakata
72 844 9000
Mon–Sun 7am–11pm

A growing amount of bookstores in Japan have become destinations in their own right, by being extraordinary feats of architecture and design, showcasing books and magazines, household products, coffee and food. Hirakata is a secret destination, a statement store for locals escaping the city on a rainy (or humid) day, who head to this book biosphere for a mini break. The building is incredible, especially at night when the inner-glow highlights the 'Jenga' style asymmetrical glass-box monolith. Explore the estimated 150,000 books (many titles are in English). Don't miss the central well, where a curated history of famous books are displayed in monolithic, floor-to-ceiling shelves. Floors are themed so the books you are hunting for can be easily found, and you'll find that they are paired with homewares, clothing, music and CDs to match the themes. A relaxed attitude means you are free to browse or sink into comfortable chairs for a good read. Cafes and bakeries make the T-Site a hard place to leave once you have settled in.

From Kitahama–Osaka station on the Keihan mainline to Hirakatashi station (20 min).

CUP NOODLES MUSEUM IKEDA

8-25 Masumicho, Ikeda, Osaka
72 752 3484
Mon–Sun 9.30am–4.30pm

Pot noodles are found in convenience stores everywhere in Japan and are the ultimate fast-food when you need a flavourful, salty hit. The IKEDA factory manufactured the first pot noodle – the chicken ramen – in 1958. It was created by Nissin' Food Product's Momofuku Ando, and a statue of him greets you outside the museum and his work shed is inside. Fun for kids and adults alike, the museum features walls and walls of pop-colour noodle pots, a noodle pot tunnel and a giant 'dissected' pot noodle (see how it works!). Don't miss the cup noodle dispensing machines and a 'tastery', where you can sample different types of cup noodles. Watch the history of the cup noodle in the plastic pot-shaped theatre. A real highlight is that you can design your own flavour and packaging – a personalised cup noodle, what a time to be alive!

From Osaka–Umeda station on the Hankyu Takarazuka line to Ikeda station (26 min).

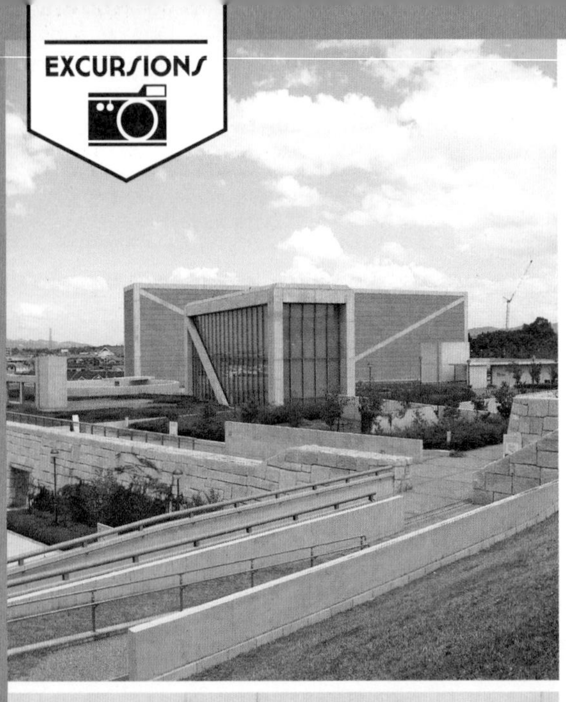

OSAKA PREFECTURAL SAYAMAIKEHAKU MUSEUM

2 Chome Ikejirinaka,
Osakasayama
72 367 8891
Tues–Sun 10am–5pm

Fans of Tadao Ando (and engineering nerds) take note! Ando has designed a museum that celebrates the Sayamaike Pond, Japan's oldest dam and waterway, whose history stretches back for over 1400 years. The water source was tended by various people over the centuries: Buddhist priests, monks and even samurai, many who spent the bulk of their lives in its service. The museum sits next to the 'pond'. It's a Brutalist concrete bunker with ramps, stairs, pockets, hollows and striking water steps, where water flows over a system of concrete gradations, much as it might in an actual dam, but more … artistically. Ando's museum in many ways resembles the tank and grate system that you would see at a dam structure. It's an amazing design, paying great homage to the history of the dam. Its exhibits throw light on a much-revered water source that continues to supply Osakasayama to this day.

From Osaka–Namba station on the Nankai Koya line express to Osakasayamashi station (36 min).

EXPO '70 COMMEMORATIVE PARK

1-1 Senribanpakukoen, Suita
6877 7387
Mon–Sun 9.30am–5pm

In 1970 the world fair was set up in this space, with 75 different pavilions, now it has over 5000 cherry blossom trees, making it one of the most popular sakura (cherry blossom) celebration sites in Osaka. Even if you're not in Japan during Hanami (cherry blossom season), the park has other attractions. Remnants of the World Fair remain and make for a fun retro stroll. They include Tarō Okamoto's Tower of the Sun, a quirky 70-metre-high (230 feet) alien sculpture. The interior, which has been refurbished and reopened to the public, features a colourful exhibition of The Tree of Life, which kids will love. The park also features several spectacular flower plantations and an impressive Japanese landscaped garden. The **Japan Folk Crafts Museum** is on the grounds and showcases a large display of ceramics, painting and textiles.

POCKET TIP

The new shopping mall Expocity (2-1 Senribanpakukoen, Suita) features Japan's biggest ferris wheel, the Redhorse Osaka Wheel, which stands at a towering 123 metres (403 feet).

From Osaka–Umeda station on the Midosuji line to Senri-Chuo station (32 min).

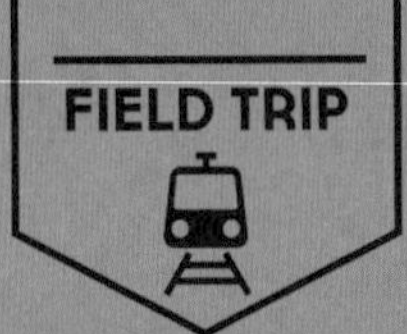

MOUNT KOYA

Koya-san, the spiritual mountain, home of Zen Buddhism and one of Japan's 'power spots', is a magical destination that should be visited with an open heart and mind. The ravages of time and onslaught of spiritual tourists have left no mark. The town is made for long walks along sacred trails, popping in and out of temples and eating handmade wagashi (Japanese sweets), which all make for contemplative explorations on hallowed grounds. If you are looking for your own enlightenment, you might be missing the point – go with a heart that searches for the peace and enlightenment of others. A selfless pilgrimage makes for the best Koya experience – and what an experience it is.

An easy daytrip from Osaka, it's still better to stay over, as a day visit won't do it justice. You can get the train from Osaka–Namba Station, then the cable car. A temple stay (*see* p. 135), in the right place and in the right frame of mind, in your preferred season, will be one of your life's most cherished memories. Vegetarian banquets, chanting monks, beautiful gardens, meditation, forested surrounds, Koya is truly the stuff of devotional Japan. In a world of noise, it is a simple, quiet break from tech, stress and the 24-hour news cycle. Why not switch off your screens for your stay and digitally declutter in this magnificent environment?

→ *Kongobuji Temple*

SIGHTS

A popular pilgrimage begins at the **Ichinohashi Bridge** – 200,000 people are interred in the area (wishing to be resting forever in such a spiritual place). The walk is accented by stone lanterns, statues and overgrown tombs. The **Gokusho Offering Hall**, **Gobyobashi Bridge** and the **Miroku Stone** (*see* p. 135) are standout features of the walk. Your ultimate destination is **Kobo Daishi's Mausoleum**, featuring the striking **Okunoin Temple**. **Garan**, the main temple complex in the town of Koya, is full of stunning temples and shrines, some wooden and darkly coloured, others vermillion red. The **Reihokan Museum** offers up a history of the area and if you need any more information ask your temple stay host or head to the **Koyasan Tourist Information Centre** on the main street.

POCKET TIP

The midnight cemetery guided tour is a must.

/LEEPING

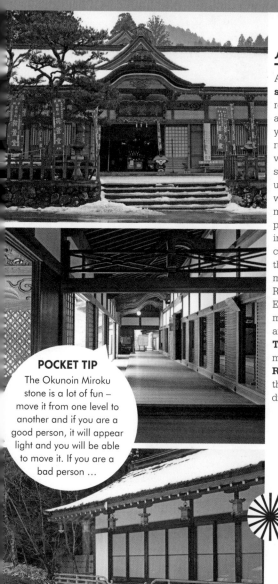

At Mount Koya, a **temple stay** gives you a bed in a real monastery – book ahead and find one that appeals, you can often get a beautiful rustic room with stunning views and maybe even a hot springs bath. If you can get up early enough, you can watch the monks at morning meditation, with chants and prayers, engulfed by swirling incense and accented by chiming bells. Be at one with the gentle lifestyle of the monks and savour the Shojin Ryori vegetarian banquet. Explore the area of your monastery to uncover beauty and treasures. **Kongobuji Temple** is the area's stunning main monastery. Its **Banrutei Rock Garden** is beautiful, the biggest of Japan's Zen dry gardens.

POCKET TIP

The Okunoin Miroku stone is a lot of fun – move it from one level to another and if you are a good person, it will appear light and you will be able to move it. If you are a bad person …

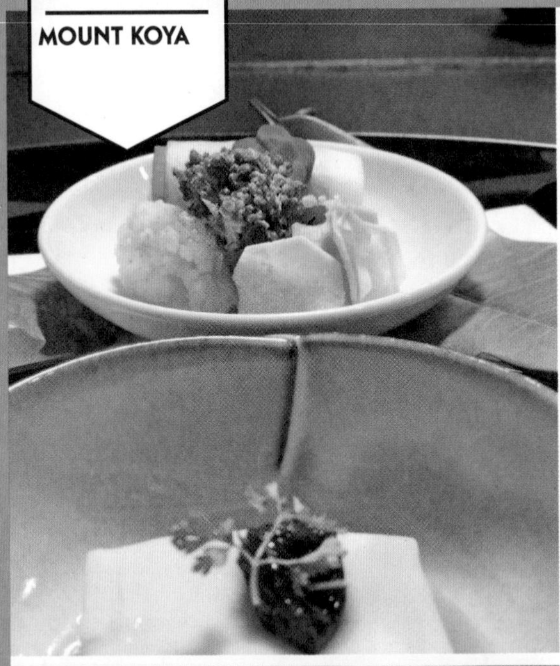

SHOPPING & EATING

If you are staying at a temple, your food will be a **Shojin Ryori** vegetarian banquet (some places serve meat and fish), made of perfect, tiny morsels of mountain vegetable tempura, pickles, mushrooms, rice, miso, tempeh, bracken starch and other treats. It's healthy, delicious and a Japanese institution that's been perfected over many years. In Koya, visitors can reserve a traditional vegetarian lunch at **Shokubo Temple** (447 Koyasan). Restaurants that all do a simple, delicious vegetarian lunch are **Sanbou** (722 Koyasan), **Bon on Shya** (767 Koyasan) and **Hanabishi** (769 Koyasan). Enquire at your temple or book ahead online.

In Koya town, **Maruman** (778 Koyasan) does a tasty lunch in a gorgeous traditional room. You'll find similar in **Kadohama Goma Tofu** (230 Koyasan). Head to **Hamadaya** (444 Koyasan) to experience the sesame seed-based tofu. You can buy it to take-away at **Morishita** (238 Koyasan).

Shopping in the area will mostly mean gathering local omiyage (regional souvenirs), gifts and mementoes. **Juzuya** (771 Koyasan) stocks wooden and pearl Juzu prayer beads, mala Buddhist bracelets and religious-themed trinkets. Our favourite store, **Nanpodo**, (807 Koyasan) has delicious local mocchi (rice flour sweets) and **Fuzen** (732 Koyasan) do one of the area's specialties: mugwort and sweet bean paste in bamboo leaves. **Kasakuni** (49 Koyasan) makes miroku-ishi, a mocchi sweet named after the famous nearby stone (*see* p. 135).

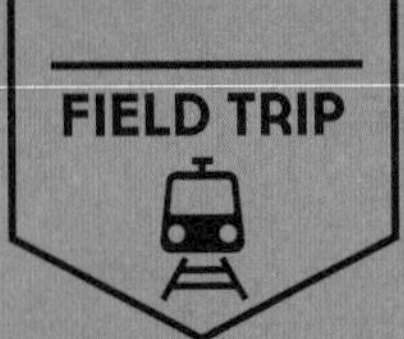

NARA

Nara is one of Japan's ancient capitals, one of the country's most beloved regions and is easily accessible from Osaka and Kyoto. It is a remarkable place, an area steeped in religious significance, with a long history of craft and a unique food palette. Nara Park (*see* p. 140) is a major tourist destination, and for good reason. The free-roaming deer make it a rare chance to stroll with adorable creatures and it is home to some of Japan's most important historical buildings and religious areas. Natural wonders also abound, such as the Nara Park Primeval Forest, a haunting glade with a plethora of botanical and entomological import finds.

The history of Nara's crafts is deep and intricate. Pottery, ceramics, wood and textiles were forged here in ancient times and are now represented in traditional shops by young creatives using handmade methods. 'Farm to table' and 'slow food' is just what they've been doing for centuries. The streets are dotted with craft, homewares and food specialty stores.

Catch the Yamatoji Rapid from Tennoji station in Osaka to Nara. It only takes 34 minutes.

→ *Kofuku-Ji*

P
空
P 有料
600

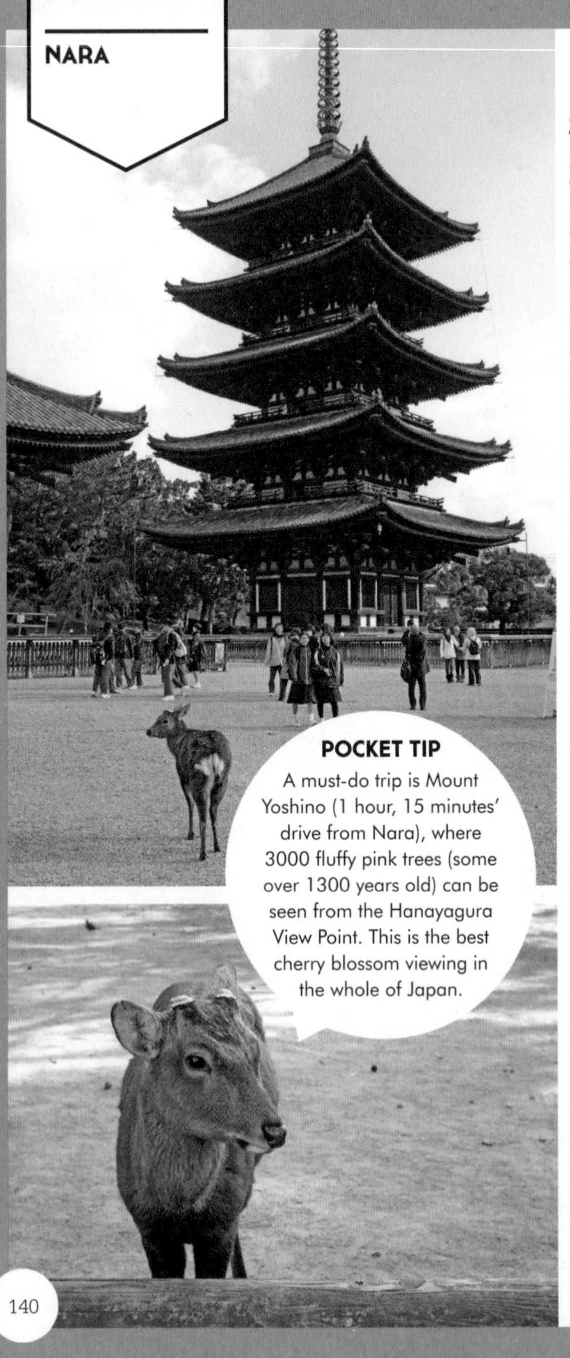

POCKET TIP

A must-do trip is Mount Yoshino (1 hour, 15 minutes' drive from Nara), where 3000 fluffy pink trees (some over 1300 years old) can be seen from the Hanayagura View Point. This is the best cherry blossom viewing in the whole of Japan.

SIGHTS

Nara's standout landmark is **Todai-ji**, one of Japan's seven great temples and the world's largest wooden structure. The temple dates back to the mid-700s and walking around it is a religious experience. Admire the towering wooden ceilings, swirling incense and Japan's largest bronze Buddha – flanked by a range of impressive statues.

Nara Park grew organically around many of Nara's famous sights but wasn't officially established until 1880. The park is populated by free-roaming deer (certified National Treasures and considered the 'messengers of the gods'), who are only too happy for you to feed them their favourite shika senbei (deer crackers) bought from park vendors. It's especially wonderful for families. Nara Park is a rare opportunity in Hanami (cherry blossom season) to see deer roaming among cherry blossoms.

Other points of interest in the park include **Kofuku-Ji**, with its impressive five-tiered pagoda, the **Nara National Museum**, housing Buddhist art and artefacts, and the **Kasuga Taisha Shrine**, with an impressive 3000 stone lanterns.

Outside of the park, **Gango-Ji** goes back to the 700s, making it one of Japan's oldest temples. Other essential

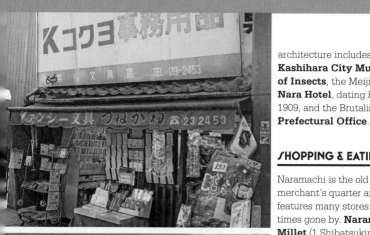

architecture includes sci-fi hive **Kashihara City Museum of Insects**, the Meiji-era **Nara Hotel**, dating back to 1909, and the Brutalist **Nara Prefectural Office**.

SHOPPING & EATING

Naramachi is the old merchant's quarter and features many stores from times gone by. **Naramachi Millet** (1 Shibatsukinukecho) is set in an old machiya (traditional wooden townhouse) and has premium pottery and local artisan crafts. **New Light Pottery** (5-1-40 Nijoojiminami) is a beautiful store that sells Hiroyuki Nagatomi's coveted designer hangings and wall lamps. For craft and homewares, head to **Kurumi-no-ki** (567-1 Horencho).

Nara excels in traditional and organic food. Head to rustic **Onwa** (3-23 Sanjoomiyacho) on the west side of Nara station, and try a vegan bowl. Delicious lunch and dinner options can also be found at rice specialist **Gohan No Aida** (12 Umematsuen). **Cherry's Spoon** (26 Nishiterabayashicho) makes rustic lunch plates, excellent coffee and sweets in a beautiful old building with tatami mats.

POCKET TIP

The Nara Craft Museum has it all in one place to peruse and buy: calligraphy tools, tea whisks, hemp cloth and the traditional Akahada pottery.

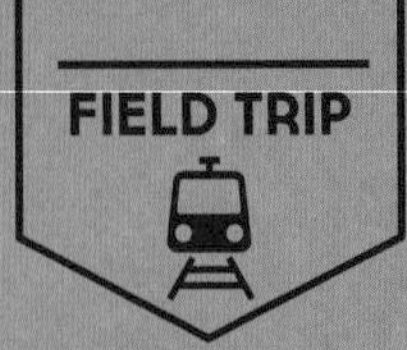

ARIMA ONSEN

One of the three oldest hot spring areas in Japan, Arima Onsen is famous for both its gold and silver water. It's an easy daytrip from Osaka, a perfect, relaxing escape and a great way to dip your toes into onsen (hot springs bath) culture. The 'gold water' is iron-rich sulphide that turns a rusty gold on contact with the air. Hot spring bathers look like they are luxuriating in baths of pure gold. Like gold, the water is truly precious, a tonic for the blood and a soothing muscle relaxant. Arima features many onsen, only accessible if you are staying at hotels or ryokan, but some, like wonderful Tosen Goshoboh (*see* p. 144), have day-rates and lunch packages. There are also two public onsen (*see* p. 144) in town, one with gold water and one with radium rich 'silver water,' which also has many healing properties.

The town of Arima Onsen is rustic and walkable, dotted with many souvenir stalls, street food vendors and delicious food opportunities. Around the town various hot springs' wells steam and spout, wafting sulphurous scents through the streets and giving it the feeling of a unique and historical resort town. Onsen towels and gold and silver bathsalts are the souvenir picks, however there so many inexpensive gifts here to take home to family and friends that you may need to have multiple onsen in-between shopping. To get here, catch a bus from Hankyu Highway in the Osaka–Umeda station terminal to Arima bus stop; it takes around one hour. You can get a shinkansen (fast train) from Shin Kobe, to Arima Onsen in 64 minutes.

→ *Bath towels in souvenir stores*

ませ

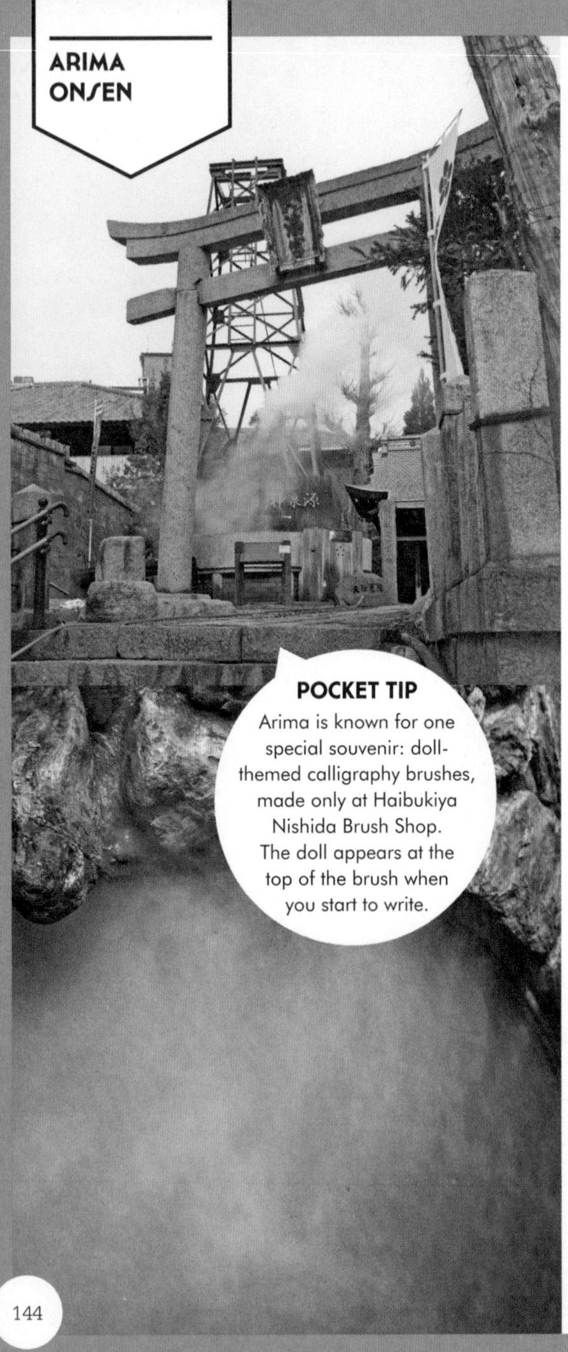

POCKET TIP

Arima is known for one special souvenir: doll-themed calligraphy brushes, made only at Haibukiya Nishida Brush Shop. The doll appears at the top of the brush when you start to write.

SIGHTS

As you head into town you'll get your first impression of Arima Onsen, a lengthy, sculptured waterway that channels water through town, past hotels and under bridges, punctuated by small gourd-shaped pools of the area's treasured gold liquid. Everything in the town is signposted, so finding the focal points is easy.

In the centre of town you'll find **Kin-no-yu**, one of Arima's two public onsen. The gold water bath is a famous spot for public bathing and the frontage features a popular gold water footbath. Walk up the winding streets past souvenir vendors and eateries, old wooden townhouses and steaming, angry hot spring sources to find the 'silver water' onsen, **Gin-no-yu**. This small and rustic onsen is popular, relaxed and has no problem with tattoos, which can often be prohibited in onsens. Other day-rate onsen include **Taiko-no-yu**, the biggest onsen in Arima and the one with the most options. At charming **Tosen Goshoboh**, men and women enter the onsen separately but can converse once inside by way of a low partition. Drop in for lunch and admire the beautiful building. The origins of the inn date back to the 1300s.

SHOPPING & EATING

Arima is a stroll around, relaxed affair, with street food galore, so pop into shops and stores that sell the local delicacies.

Mitsomori (290-1 Arimacho, Kita-ku, Kobe) dates back to 1907, has ten stores in town and sells Arima's famous spicy onsen cracker: tansan senbei, which they still make by hand. They also make mountain yam and brown sugar maju (steamed buns). You can also buy the crackers and a range of steamed manju at **Arima Senbei**'s main store. Other local food specialties include arima roll cake and tanba black bean pie. Most menus feature the area's famed Kobe beef and 80-year-old **Takenaka Butchers** does a great Kobe beef croquette. A delicious lunch at **Tosen Goshoboh** (*see* p. 144) before an onsen soak is heaven. **Yoshitakaya** (259 Arimacho, Kita-ku, Kobe) sells some of Arima's famous products: bath salts (create your own gold or silver bath!), handcream, soap, skincare and the area's famous 'Teppo' water – a hot springs' cider that has been in production since the 1900s.

GETTING TO OSAKA

KANSAI INTERNATIONAL AIRPORT (KIX)

Train

The Limited Express Haruka for Shin-Osaka station and Tennoji station takes 45–60 minutes for around ¥1800–2400.

Kansai Airport Rapid Service for Osaka and Tennoji station takes 65–70 minutes for around ¥1200.

The Nankai Limited Airport Express Rapi:t for Nankai Namba station takes 37 minutes for around ¥1300, stopping at limited stations. There is also an express version of this train that is a little cheaper but takes a little longer.

Taxi

It takes around 50 minutes to Osaka–Umeda or Namba stations and costs over ¥20,000 (this is a very expensive option).

Kate Bus to Umeda Station

It takes 78 minutes and costs ¥1550 one-way, ¥2200 return.

Shuttle services

There are multiple shuttle options, depending on where you are staying. Check: airportshuttles.com/osaka.php

HARUKA & ICOCA

Discount train tickets from Kansai International Airport cost around ¥3300 one-way and ¥4600 return.

Exchanging your Japan Rail pass in the Osaka Area

The Japan Rail pass is a set time train ticket you can buy online outside of Japan that works out as an effective and cheap way to ride on the Shinkansen and all JR trains. You can exchange at:

Kansai Airport ticket office.

Shin-Osaka station at JR ticket offices, JR West and JR Central, JR Tokai Tours Shin-Osaka Office (Travel Service Center Shin-Osaka station).

Osaka station at Ticket Office (Central No.12,13), Nippon Travel Agency TiS Osaka Branch (Travel Service Center Osaka).

GETTING AROUND

OSAKA TRAVEL PASSES

All passes can (and should) be purchased online outside of Japan. Until March 2021 (at this stage) passes can be bought in Japan but cost 20% more.

Osaka Amazing Pass

This one- or two-day pass gives you unlimited train and bus travel and discounts at sights. It costs ¥2700–¥3600. Discounted entry includes: Osaka Castle Museum, Osaka Science Museum, Umeda Sky Building Floating Garden Observatory (*see* p. 2) and more. See: osaka-info.jp/en/page/travel-passes

Suica, Pasmo & Icoca cards

A convenient option that lets you ride on private railways, JR trains, some buses and also to buy things in convenience stores.

Grab a **Suica**, **Pasmo** or **Icoca** card from machines at train stations. For a deposit of ¥500 (redeemable at the end of your trip), these cards are rechargeable and easy to use. Top them up at the machines (they have English instructions) and swipe them at the barrier gates to get into a station.

You can use these cards throughout Japan, making them the best choice if you are travelling from city to city.

Yokoso! Osaka Ticket

A one-day ticket for international visitors to use for trains and buses in Osaka. It costs ¥1500–1650, you can buy from a travel agency in your home country, at Kansai Airport or online. See: howto-osaka.com/en/ticket/ticket/yokoso.html

Osaka one- and two-day passes

For use on all buses and trains for one or two days. It costs ¥700–1300, you can buy from a travel agency in your home country or at Kansai Airport. See: subway.osakametro.co.jp/en/guide/fare/planned_ticket/otoku-joshaken_tsunen.php

Keihan Osaka & Kyoto pass

Private train pass, costs ¥800–1200. See: www.keihan.co.jp/travel/en/tickets/special/

KANSAI-WIDE PASSES

JR Kansai Passes

See: westjr.co.jp/global/en/ticket/pass/kansai/

Kansai One Pass

A one-day pass. It costs ¥3000 and includes travel in the whole Kansai region (excludes some private railways). See: kansaionepass.com

Kansai Area Pass

A one-, two-, three- or four-day pass. It costs ¥2200–6500 and includes airport travel, and travel to Kyoto, Nara, Wakayama, Kobe and more.

Kansai Wide Area Pass

A five-day pass for the widest area of travel, including Okayama, Kurashiki, Kinosaki hot springs and Shirahama hot springs. It costs around ¥9000.

Kansai-Hiroshima Area Pass

A five-day pass, including to Okayama and Hiroshima. It costs around ¥13,500.

TRANSPORT TO MOUNT KOYA

Koyasan-World Heritage Ticket

A two-day pass. It costs from ¥2900 and can be purchased at Osaka–Namba station or online. See: howto-osaka.com/en/ticket/ticket/koyasan.html

Taxis

Taxis cost ¥660 for the first two kilometres, then ¥80 for every 300 metres after that. Late at night, fares can rise by 20%. All tolls will be calculated in the cost of your fare.

Bikes

Riding a bike is a great way to get around a single precinct. Osaka has rental 'ports' in and around the city, so that you can pick up a bike at one port and drop it at another, there are also bike share and community bike programs. Great resources online are:

rentabikeosaka.com

docomo-cycle.jp/osaka

cycleosaka.com

hubchari.com/en

Buses

Osaka buses have a flat fee of ¥210, you enter and pay the driver through the front door. It's best to have the exact change when paying, or use your Suica, Pasmo or Icoca card (*see* p. 146).

Walking

Osaka is a relatively easy city to walk around, especially if you plan your day visiting precincts that are next to each other. It's a city where we don't seem to use the train as much as in other big cities. Remember, walking will help you to really get to know the city, happen upon things you were not expecting, and find interesting and unusual scenes, people and sights. It's also really good for you!

MONEY

Japan's currency is the yen, denoted by ¥. It comes in denominations of ¥1000, ¥2000, ¥5000 and ¥10,000 in notes, and ¥1, ¥5, ¥10, ¥50, ¥100 and ¥500 in coins. The ¥5 and ¥50 coins have holes in the middle of them. There is a 10% consumption tax in Japan. It is sometimes included in the price of things but often isn't, so check first. Sometimes a service charge is also added, so for hotels and restaurants this can really stack up. Make sure you're aware of any additional costs like this before purchasing something. Not all cash machines (ATMs) take international cards so if you need to get extra cash look for a **Seven Bank**, which will always accept them. You'll find Seven Banks in **7-Elevens** and in separate outlets. Some large stores, department stores and main post offices have international ATMs.

LOCKERS

Lockers are a staple at every train station. Small, medium and large sizes are available and prices start from ¥300.

Both Osaka–Umeda and Shin–Osaka stations have luggage rooms for larger or longer-term storage. Both are located on the first floor and they have set opening times, so please take note and pick up your bags while they are still open.

PHONES & WI-FI

To access wi-fi in Osaka, you have a few options. Many travellers rent pocket wi-fi at Kansai International Airport to use with their smart phone. You can also hire a mobile phone at the airport, or buy a SIM card for your phone at outlets around the city, such as **SoftBank** or **Docomo**, Osaka's major mobile phone providers. **7-Eleven** stores have free wi-fi, as do **Loft** department stores. Check online before you leave for some great new apps to download that find hotspots for you.

Osaka Free wi-fi is available all over the city at hotspots, translations, major tourist attractions and popular hubs. You must log in every half hour, however there is no time limit. Look for the maroon Osaka Free wi-fi sign.

JR West Free Wi-Fi service is available at some of the big stations, again you'll need to sign in to use. If you search for pocket wi-fi online, you'll see the myriad of choices, many have cheaper deals if you book online. Some hotels now provide pocket wi-fi or a smart phone in the room so remember to ask before you book, it may make a difference to your choice.

To call somewhere outside of Osaka, dial 010, then the country code of where you're calling, and then the area code, dropping the initial '0'. Osaka's area code is 66, but you don't need to dial it if you're calling within Osaka.

It's considered rude to talk on your mobile phone on trains.

BINS & RECYCLING

Consider buying some reusable chopsticks and taking a reusable water bottle and container, so you don't use too many single-use items.

Bins are not that common so when you see one dispose of your rubbish. When you find a bin it will often have all the recycle options.

Bins are divided into:

PET bottles (yellow)

Combustible/burnable rubbish (red)

Bottles and cans (blue)

Plastics (green)

HOTEL RECOMMENDATIONS

Capsules

9 Hours, First Cabin, Cabin & Capsule Hotel J-Ship Namba, New Japan Capsule Hotel Cabana (male only)

Hostels

Osaka Guest House Midoriya, The Dorm Hostel, Drop Inn Osaka, Hostel Wasabi

Well priced

Cinnamon Hotel, The Blend Inn – Studio

Hotel with onsen or sento

Mitsui Garden Hotel Osaka Premier, Onyado Nono Namba Hot Springs, Spa World

Boutique

Hotel The Flag Shinsaibashi, Hotel Yu-shu, Nest Hotel

Ryokan

Hokousou, Osaka Yamatoya Honten

Just out of town, beautiful ryokan experiences

Amami Onsen Nanten-en, Minoo Kanko Hotel, Minoo Onsen Spa Garden

SHOPPING

When you enter a shop (or restaurant), staff will say 'irrashaimase' (you are welcome). There's not really an answer to this, but sometimes it's so emphatic you'll feel like saying something in return! Just say 'konnichiwa' (hello).

SHOPPING TIPS

Carry your passport with you so that if you purchase something worth over ¥10,000 in major department stores or stores that have a tax-free sign, it can be bought duty-free.

Do not haggle in Osaka, unless you are at an open-air market.

The consumption tax is now 10% and will often be added to prices at payment. Many shops have a tax-back service, if you'd like peace of mind getting your tax back. Most big department stores offer it but not all small shops do.

ELECTRONICS

Osaka has great electronic gadgets and devices, but remember that they are a different wattage and the power plugs use different outlets. If you really have to buy something, you'll need to get it converted or buy a transformer device. Some stores will sell western versions, which have already been changed over. Duty-free places at the airport will have western-style wattage.

EATING OUT

Make sure you check the opening hours of your desired cafe or restaurant. Most cafes and bars shut for one day during the week, and many cafes open around 11am or 12pm.

Lunch starts at 11.30am and finishes between 2 and 3pm.

Lunch-sets are great value, especially at places that do an expensive dinner.

It's good fun to try the omakase (chef's choice) at restaurants. The chefs decide what they think is the best choice for you.

Many small eateries have plastic food models out the front of their establishment, and many cafes have pictorial menus, which is very handy if you don't speak Japanese. You can show a staff member the menu, point to your preferred dish and say either 'onegaishimasu' (polite) or 'okudasai' – two Japanese words for 'please'.

If you don't speak Japanese, ask your hotel to make restaurant reservations on your behalf.

Most places are licensed.

When using chopsticks, don't stick them upright in a bowl of rice – this is a funeral custom. Also, don't pass food to, or take food from other people using chopsticks, and don't spear food with them (okay, we may have done this a few times …). Lastly, don't use chopsticks to move a bowl towards you.

It is customary to pour other people's drinks.

Tipping is not a thing in Osaka. In fact, it will cause confusion.

MANNERS

Manners are very important in Japan, so always be as polite as possible. Invoke your inner sense of calm and treat everyone with respect, and respect will be returned to you. The deeper someone bows, the more respect they are showing you. Most younger people don't bow as much now, but a slight bow of the head is always a good thing.

Take off your shoes before getting onto a tatami mat or entering a house. A lot of restaurants will also require you to remove your shoes, but the staff will let you know. There are usually slippers provided, but these are for going to the bathroom (you don't have to worry about this in more contemporary restaurants). You should even take your shoes off when entering a clothing-store changing room.

If you're sick with a cold, buy a face mask. Also, don't take a wet umbrella into a shop; use the bags or holders provided. (Note: grab a clear plastic umbrella from konbinis (stands) at the train stations if it's raining; they are cheap and well made.)

Crime is low in Japan, generally. There are very few dangerous areas. Honestly, you could drop your wallet and someone will pick it up and give it back to you, or if you left it somewhere, it will likely be mailed to you.

USEFUL WORDS & PHRASES

Pronunciation is simply this: vowels are 'a' (pronounced like the 'u' in up), 'i' (pronounced like the 'i' in imp), 'u' (pronounced as the 'oo' in book), 'e' (pronounced as the 'e' in egg) and 'o' (pronounced as the 'o' in lock). This doesn't change for any word, and if two vowels are placed together, you say them as if they were separate vowel sounds in a row. Simple! The letter 'r' is pronounced as a cross between an 'r' and an 'l'; the easiest way to make this sound is to touch the roof of your mouth with the tip of your tongue.

Useful Kanji

Osaka: 大阪
Japan: 日本
Yen: 円
Male: 男
Female: 女
Enter: 入口
Exit: 出口
North: 北
South: 南
East: 東
West: 西

Try and memorise the Kanji for Osaka; it's especially useful for reading the weather on television. Male and female Kanji is also useful for toilet signage in some restaurants and cafes.

Do you speak English?: anata wa eigo o hanashimasu ka?
I don't understand: wakarimasen
I don't understand Japanese: Nihongo ga wakarimasen
Hello: konnichiwa
Good morning: ohayou gozaimasu
Goodnight: oyasuminasai
Goodbye: sayonara
See you later: mata ne
Nice to meet you: hajimemashite
Please: kudasai/onegaishimasu
Thank you: arigato, arigato gozaimasu
Thank you very much: domo arigato
Excuse me: sumimasen
How are you?: genki desu ka?
I'm well: genki desu or genki
How much is this?: ikura desu ka?
I'll take this: kore kudasai
Cheers!: kanpai!
I would like a beer please: biru wo kudasai (or add 'nama' before 'biru' for a draught beer)
Delicious: oishii
Can I have the bill please?: okanjo onegaishimasu?
After eating a delicious meal say: gochisousama deshita
Train station: eki
Airport: kuukou
Taxi: takushi
I love Japan!: Watashi wa Nihon ga daisuki!

Kansai language (dialect) or Kasai Ben

Thank you: ookini
Hello: maido
Goodbye: sainara
Welcome: oideyasu
Very: metcha, ie metcha oishii, metcha metcha kawaii
How much? nambo?
So-so: bochi bochi

CONVENIENCE STORES

Osaka's convenience stores (konbinis) are awesome. You might be used to convenience stores having higher prices for junky products, but in Osaka they are fast, cheap, convenient and sell great stuff, including cheap beer, fresh fruit and vegetables, sweets, magazines and delicious take-away food. Sometimes they have their own select ranges, and FamilyMarts stock Muji products. You can even buy concert and museum tickets. We could happily do a convenience-store tour of Osaka. FamilyMart, Lawson, Daily Yamazaki and 7-Eleven are the main stores but look out for cute neighbourhood versions too.

VENDING MACHINES

Vending machines are everywhere. The variety of drinks Japan has is staggering – convenient if you want a hot green tea or coffee in winter, or a cold drink at any time of the year. Vending machines can also sell anything from hamburgers to toilet paper, stationery, shirts, alcohol and cup noodles.

TOILETS

Public toilets are easy to find and range from the basic to the so-intricate that you'll never have time to work out all of the functions. Some toilets play music, so pick a tune! The nicest toilets are located in department stores. Some public toilets are non-western (squat) ones, so beware, or dare!

PUBLIC HOLIDAYS & FESTIVALS

Christmas Day is a normal working day in Osaka. Christmas night is considered 'date night' in Japan, especially for the young.

New Year is the big holiday in Japan. Celebrations involve visits to shrines to pray for good fortune and health in the coming year. Businesses can close the week before New Year, and stay shut for the first few weeks of January. Check attractions before you visit.

Golden Week starts at the end of April or early May (check japan-guide.com for exact dates). Book your accommodation well in advance at this time.

BASEBALL

Baseball is a completely Japanese experience, with crazy die-hard fans, beer and fun snack foods. The Osaka team is the ORIX Buffaloes and plays at the **Kyocera Osaka Dome** stadium (2-1 3-chome Chiyozaki, Nishi), an impressive modern building, with capacity just under 40,000 people, that has been compared to a giant spaceship. The regional team is the Hanshin Tigers, who are from Nishinomiya, Hyōgo, and also use this stadium as their home ground.

The season runs from late March to October. Many matches start around 6pm and it's best to get there at least half an hour before starting time. A match is around three hours and 15 minutes.

Tickets can be bought at the stadium, however public holidays and weekends may be sold out. Ask at your accommodation for advice or help with booking, or try the website: govoyagin.com. Tickets are ¥1000–150000. If you want to support the local Osaka team, make sure you sit with their fans!

There are infield seats (quieter atmosphere) and outfield seats (a little more loose, out with the fans).

To access the stadium:

Dome-mae Chiyozaki station: Hanshin Namba line, exit 1

Taisho station: Osaka loop line, exit 4 (7 minutes' walk)

Kujō station: Osaka Metro, Osaka Metro Chuō line, Hanshin Electric Railway, exit 2 (13 minutes' walk).

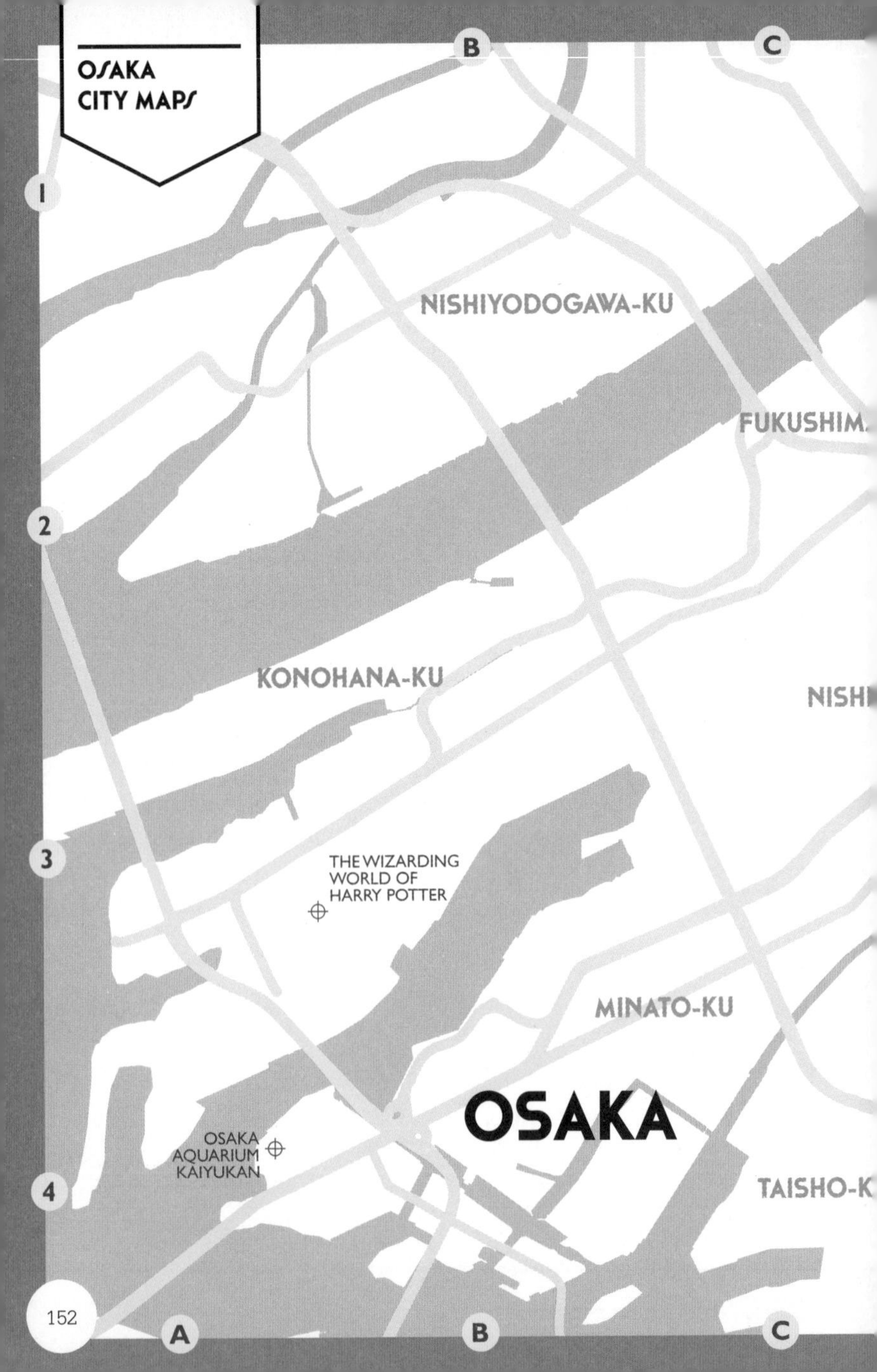
OSAKA CITY MAPS
NISHIYODOGAWA-KU
FUKUSHIM
KONOHANA-KU
NISH
THE WIZARDING WORLD OF HARRY POTTER
MINATO-KU
OSAKA
OSAKA AQUARIUM KAIYUKAN
TAISHO-K
A
B
C
1
2
3
4

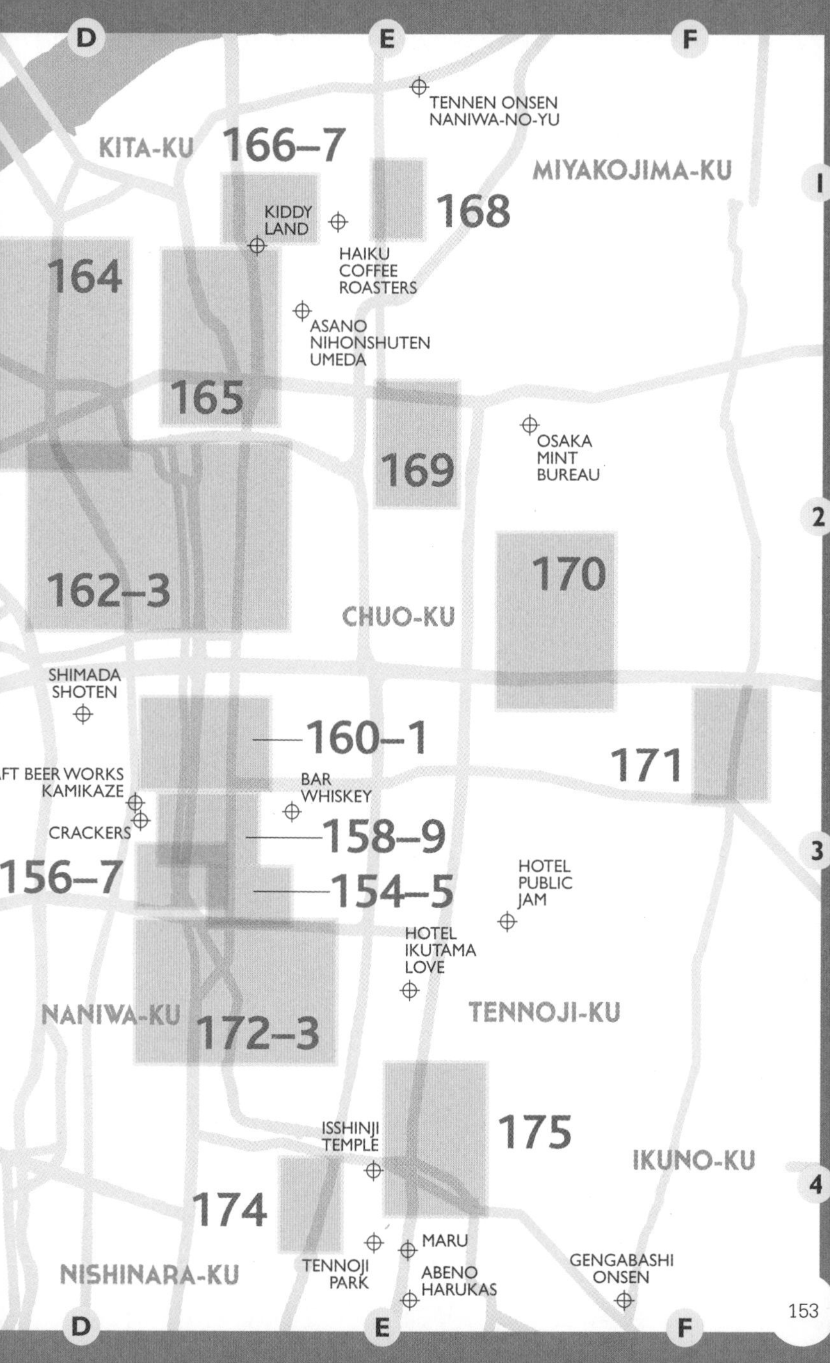
D
E
F
TENNEN ONSEN NANIWA-NO-YU
KITA-KU
166–7
MIYAKOJIMA-KU
1
KIDDY LAND
168
HAIKU COFFEE ROASTERS
164
ASANO NIHONSHUTEN UMEDA
165
OSAKA MINT BUREAU
169
2
170
162–3
CHUO-KU
SHIMADA SHOTEN
160–1
171
AFT BEER WORKS KAMIKAZE
BAR WHISKEY
CRACKERS
158–9
3
156–7
154–5
HOTEL PUBLIC JAM
HOTEL IKUTAMA LOVE
NANIWA-KU
172–3
TENNOJI-KU
175
ISSHINJI TEMPLE
IKUNO-KU
4
174
MARU
NISHINARA-KU
TENNOJI PARK
ABENO HARUKAS
GENGABASHI ONSEN
D
E
F

A
B
C
1
2
3
4
SHINSAIBASHISUJI
FamilyMart
NISHISHINSAIBASHI
MIDOSUJI
Cross Hotel Osaka
SHINSAIBASHI-SUJI
OUI
FamilyMart
SOEMONCHO
SOEMONCHO
Lawson
Shinebisu Bridge
Dotonbori-gawa
Ebisubashi Bridge
GLICO MAN SIGN
SEXMACHINE
DOTONBORI
DOTONBORI
FamilyMart
Osaka Shochiku Theatre
MATTARI PURIN
EBISUBASHI-SUJI
TSURUGI
Osaka Metro Midosuji Line
HOZENJI
KOISAN
AJINOYA
ONION STAGE KARAOKE
CRAFT BEER GULP
FamilyMart
NANBA
NAMBA HIPS
Lawson
SENNICHIMAE-DORI
SENNICHIMAE-DORI
NAMBA
Y15
S16
M20
Osaka Metro Sennichimae Line

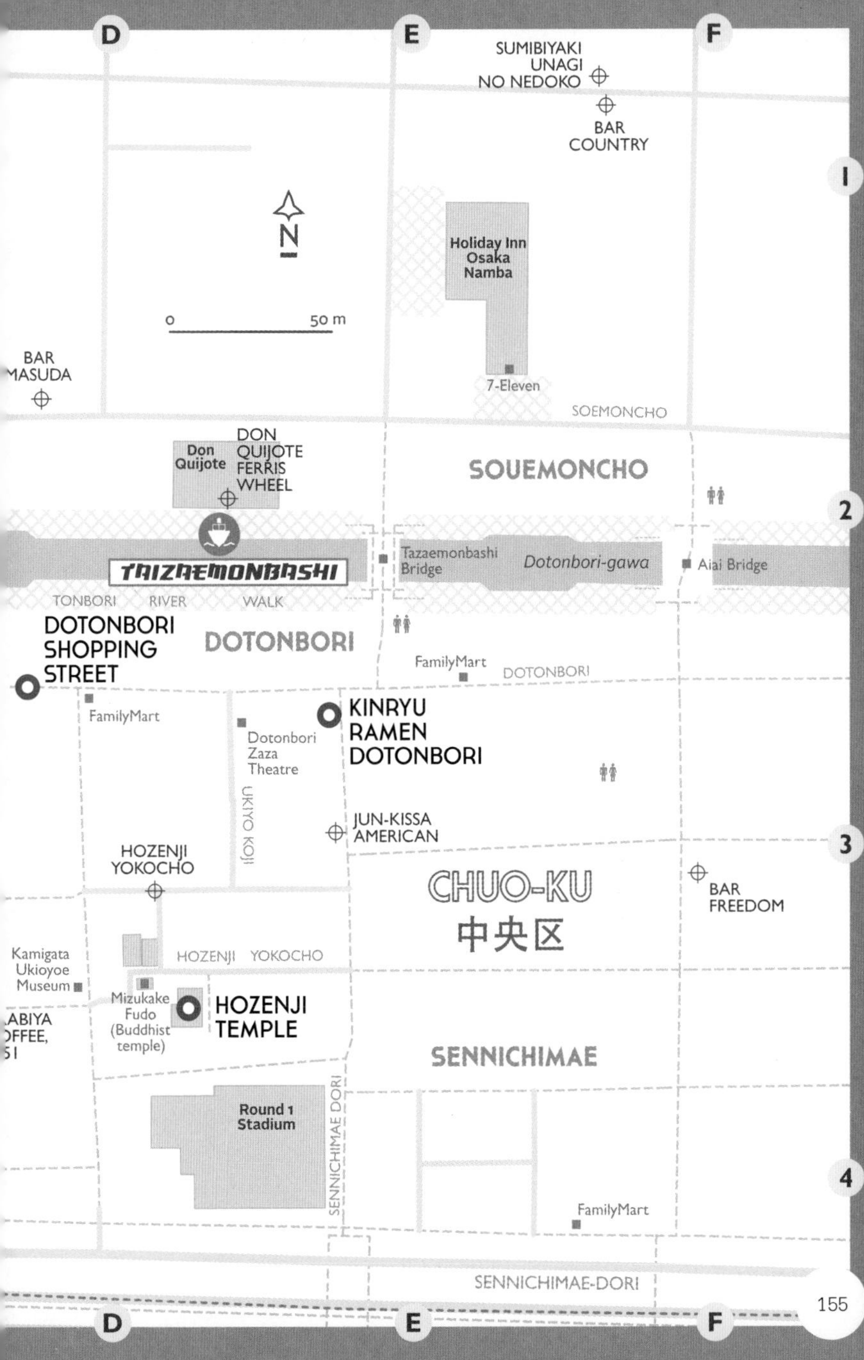
D
E
F
SUMIBIYAKI
UNAGI
NO NEDOKO
BAR
COUNTRY
I
N
Holiday Inn
Osaka
Namba
0
50 m
BAR
MASUDA
7-Eleven
SOEMONCHO
DON
QUIJOTE
FERRIS
WHEEL
Don
Quijote
SOUEMONCHO
2
TAIZAEMONBASHI
Tazaemonbashi
Bridge
Dotonbori-gawa
Aiai Bridge
TONBORI RIVER WALK
DOTONBORI
SHOPPING
STREET
DOTONBORI
FamilyMart
DOTONBORI
FamilyMart
KINRYU
RAMEN
DOTONBORI
Dotonbori
Zaza
Theatre
UKIYO KOJI
JUN-KISSA
AMERICAN
3
HOZENJI
YOKOCHO
CHUO-KU
中央区
BAR
FREEDOM
HOZENJI YOKOCHO
Kamigata
Ukioyoe
Museum
Mizukake
Fudo
(Buddhist
temple)
HOZENJI
TEMPLE
SENNICHIMAE
Round 1
Stadium
SENNICHIMAE DORI
4
FamilyMart
SENNICHIMAE-DORI
D
E
F

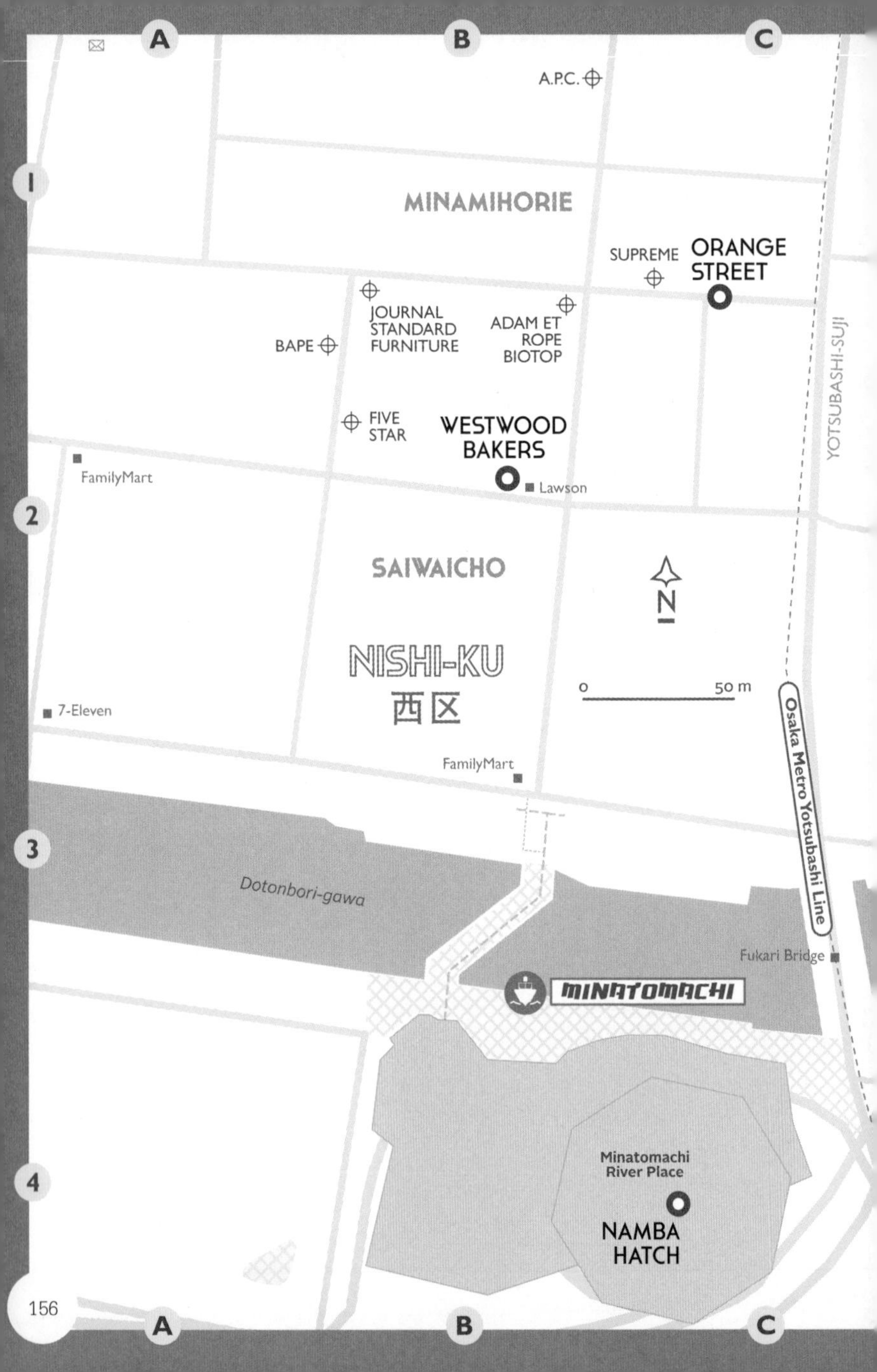
A
B
C
1
2
3
4
A.P.C.
MINAMIHORIE
SUPREME
ORANGE STREET
JOURNAL STANDARD FURNITURE
ADAM ET ROPE BIOTOP
BAPE
FIVE STAR
WESTWOOD BAKERS
YOTSUBASHI-SUJI
FamilyMart
Lawson
SAIWAICHO
N
NISHI-KU
西区
0
50 m
7-Eleven
FamilyMart
Osaka Metro Yotsubashi Line
Dotonbori-gawa
Fukari Bridge
MINATOMACHI
Minatomachi River Place
NAMBA HATCH
A
B
C

D
E
F
HANSHIN EXPRESSWAY NO. 1 LOOP ROUTE
ANGE
1
LONG SOFTCREAM
TIME BOMB RECORDS
FamilyMart
SUN BOWL SHINSAIBASHI BUILDING
Dormy Inn Shinsaibashi
Capsule Hotel Asahi Plaza
ALICE ON WEDNESDAY
CHUO-KU
中央区
NEKO NO JIKAN
GROOVENUT
2
NISHISHINSAIBASHI
SPACE STATION
Familymart
FamilyMart
HOKKYOKUSEI SHINSAIBASHI
ROR Comedy Club
APA Hotel Namba Shinsaibashi
OUI
7 Eleven
SOEMONCHO
FamilyMart
3
Lawson 100
Daikoku Bridge
Dotonbori-gawa
Shinebisu Bridge
SEXMACHINE
Lawson
DOTONBORI
DOTONBORI
4
TSURUGI
D
E
F

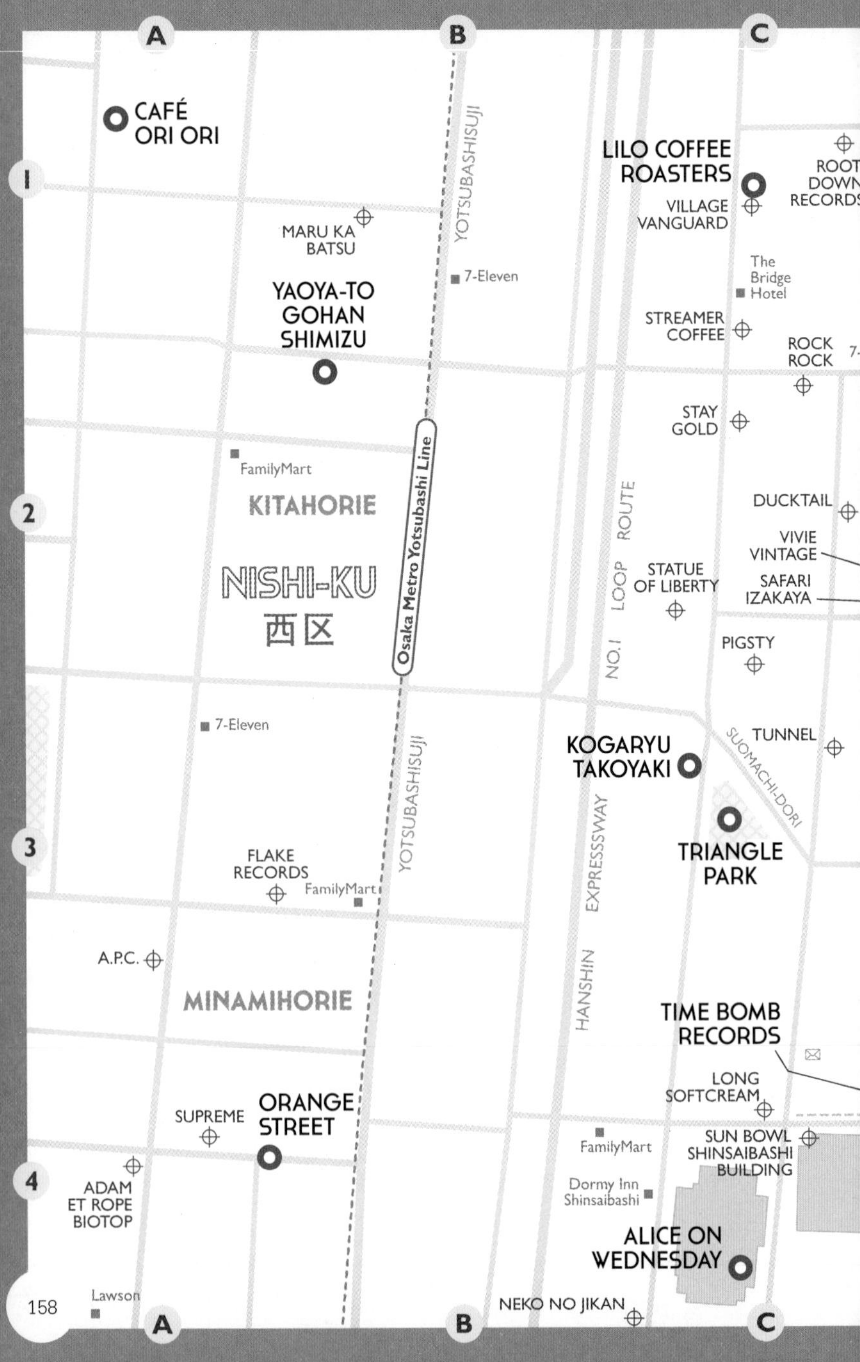
A
B
C
1
2
3
4
CAFÉ ORI ORI
LILO COFFEE ROASTERS
ROOT DOWN RECORDS
VILLAGE VANGUARD
MARU KA BATSU
YOTSUBASHISUJI
7-Eleven
The Bridge Hotel
YAOYA-TO GOHAN SHIMIZU
STREAMER COFFEE
ROCK ROCK
STAY GOLD
Osaka Metro Yotsubashi Line
FamilyMart
KITAHORIE
DUCKTAIL
VIVIE VINTAGE
NO.1 LOOP ROUTE
NISHI-KU
西区
STATUE OF LIBERTY
SAFARI IZAKAYA
PIGSTY
7-Eleven
TUNNEL
SUOMACHI-DORI
KOGARYU TAKOYAKI
TRIANGLE PARK
HANSHIN EXPRESSWAY
FLAKE RECORDS
FamilyMart
A.P.C.
MINAMIHORIE
TIME BOMB RECORDS
LONG SOFTCREAM
SUPREME
ORANGE STREET
SUN BOWL SHINSAIBASHI BUILDING
FamilyMart
ADAM ET ROPE BIOTOP
Dormy Inn Shinsaibashi
ALICE ON WEDNESDAY
Lawson
NEKO NO JIKAN

D
E
F
NISHISHINSAIBASHI
UNAGIDANI MINAMI-DORI
FamilyMart
UNAGIDANI MINAMI-DORI
Hotel Nikko Osaka
MIDOSUJI
Daimaru Shinsaibashi North
LAW CLOUD TEMPLE
FamilyMart
DAIHOJI-DORI
ARE
ROOVE
Shinsaibashi OPA
Osaka Metro Midosuji Line
ISE EBIYA
NAGAMOCHIYA
L:A BRUKET
NEEDLE TO LEAF
SHINSAIBASHI DAIMARU
FamilyMart
DAIMARU FOOD HALL
POKEMON CENTER
SHABUTEI SHINSAIBASHI
FamilyMart
CAT
INJI USED
CLOTHING
Hearton Hotel Shinsaibashi
Daimaru Shinsaibashi South
MEIJIKEN
IG STEP
SHINSAIBASHISUJI
KING KONG RECORDS
FIRST
McDonald's
SUOMACHI-DORI
CREATIVE LAMP POSTS
PEACE ON EARTH
CLAPPER
CHUO-KU
中央区
MIDOSUJI
ANGE
LILO COFFEE KISSA
N
0
50 m
SHINSAIBASHI SUJI
1
2
3
4

A
B
C
ITACHIBORI
1
0
100 m
N
ORIX Theater
Osaka Metro Yotsubashi Line
YOTSUBASHISUJI
2
Shinmachi Kita Koen
MOCHISHO
SHIZUKU
SHINMACHI
LOOP ROUTE
SHIZEN BAR
PAPRIKA
SHOKUDO
HANSHIN EXPRESSWAY NO.1
NISHI-KU
西区
Lawson
FamilyMart
3
SHINMACHI
YOTSUBASHISUJI
SATURDAYS
NYC
NAGAHORI-DORI
Osaka Metro Nagahori Tsurumi-ryokuchi Line
4
NISHIOHASHI
N14
NAGAHORI-DORI
YOTSUBASHI
Y14
FamilyMart
A
B
C

D
E
F
TOFU RYORI SORANO MINAMISEMBA
MINAMIKYUHOJIMACHI
I
Namba Shrine
7 Eleven
FamilyMart
MIDOSUJI
DOBUIKESUJI
BAKUROMACHI
McDonalds
Burger King
2
ACORN VINTAGE
FamilyMart
Osaka Metro Midosuji Line
TORISOBA ZAGIN NIBOSHI
ESPECIAL RECORDS
FamilyMart
WAD OMOTENASHI
Daiso
CHUO-KU
中央区
3
7-Eleven
ISSEY
YAKE
EMBA
FamilyMart
MILL POUR
MINAMISENBA
MIDOSUJI
Subway
Shinsaibashi-suji Shopping Arcade
FamilyMart
Lawson
Lawson
TOKYU HANDS
SHINSAIBASHI
N15
M19
4
NAGAHORI-DORI
NAGAHORI-DORI
D
E
F

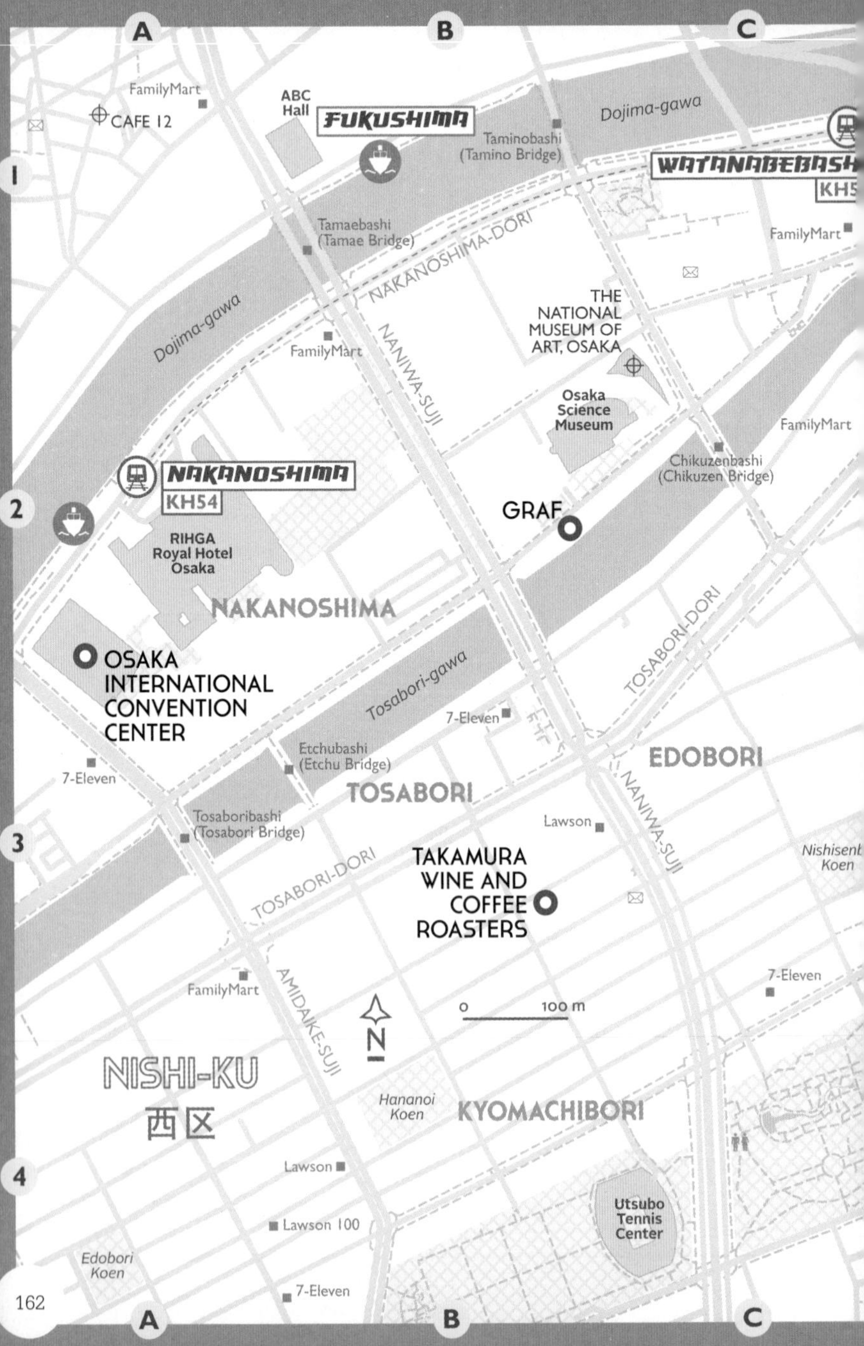
A
B
C
1
2
3
4
FamilyMart
CAFE 12
ABC Hall
FUKUSHIMA
Dojima-gawa
Taminobashi (Tamino Bridge)
WATANABEBASHI
KH5
Tamaebashi (Tamae Bridge)
NAKANOSHIMA-DORI
FamilyMart
THE NATIONAL MUSEUM OF ART, OSAKA
Dojima-gawa
FamilyMart
NANIWA-SUJI
Osaka Science Museum
FamilyMart
Chikuzenbashi (Chikuzen Bridge)
NAKANOSHIMA
KH54
GRAF
RIHGA Royal Hotel Osaka
NAKANOSHIMA
OSAKA INTERNATIONAL CONVENTION CENTER
Tosabori-gawa
TOSABORI-DORI
7-Eleven
Etchubashi (Etchu Bridge)
EDOBORI
7-Eleven
TOSABORI
NANIWA-SUJI
Tosaboribashi (Tosabori Bridge)
Lawson
TAKAMURA WINE AND COFFEE ROASTERS
Nishisenb Koen
TOSABORI-DORI
FamilyMart
AMIDAIKE-SUJI
0
100 m
N
7-Eleven
NISHI-KU
西区
Hananoi Koen
KYOMACHIBORI
Lawson
Utsubo Tennis Center
Lawson 100
Edobori Koen
7-Eleven

D
E
F
Keihan Nakanoshima Line
OEBASHI
KH52
NAKANOSHIMA DORI
Nakanoshima Festival Tower
Osaka City Hall
Osaka City Central Public Hall
1
Tosabori-gawa
Higobashi (Higo Bridge)
Yodoyabashi (Yodoya Bridge)
YODOYABASHI
KH01
Keihan Main Line
TOSABORI-DORI
KITAHAMA
HIGOBASHI
Y12
YODOYABASHI
M17
UCHIKITAHAMA-DORI
UCHIKITAHAMA-DORI
Hotel Cordia Osaka
FamilyMart
IMABASHI-DORI
SANKYUBASHI-SUJI STREET
2
UKIYOKOJI
IMABASHI-DORI
UKIYOKOJI
Osaka Metro Yotsubashi Line
7-Eleven
FamilyMart
KORAIBASHI-DORI
CHUO-KU
中央区
Lawson
SHIBAKAWA BUILDING
Osaka Metro Midosuji Line
MIDO-SUJI
LOOP ROUTE
SANKYUBASHI-SUJI
MOLE AND HOSOI COFFEES, SCENE, RICORDO & YUMIKO IIHOSHI
HIRANOMACHI
FamilyMart
7-Eleven
3
GORYO-JINJA SHRINE
FamilyMart
YUKI MUSEUM OF ART
7-Eleven
OSTEC Exhibition Hall
AWAJIMACHI
YOTSUBASHISUJI
7-Eleven
DOBUIKESUJI
SANKYUBASHI-SUJI
FamilyMart
4
HONMACHI
AZUCHIMACHI
FamilyMart
Lawson
D
E
F

A
B
C
1
2
3
4
NEW SATOYAMA
WALL OF HOPE
WILLER
FLOATING GARDEN OBSERVATORY
TAKIMIKOJI
OYODONAKA
Oyodonaka Koen
SHIN UMEDA CITY
The Westin Osaka
UMEDA SKY BUILDING
AMIDAIKE-SUJI
KITA-KU
北区
Oyodominami Koen
NANIWA SUJI
Urae Koen
The Symphony Hall
Kamifukushima Kita Koen
Daiwa Royal Hotel D-City
JR Kobe Line
JR Takarazuka Line
HANSHIN EXPRESSWAY ROUTE 11
FUKUSHIMA
JR Osaka Loop Line
GATE TOWER BUILDING
The Ritz-Carlton
Kamifukushima Koen
FUKUSHIMA-KU
福島区
FUKUSHIMA
O12
HS02
Nishi Umeda Park
Hanshin Main Line
SONEZAKI-DORI
JR Tozai Line
PIT MASTER VAMOS BBQ
ESSENTIAL STORE
SALMONBAL PARTIA
N
Fukushima Tenmangu Shrine
0
100 m
H45
SHIN FUKUSHIMA
CAFE 12
FOUJITA
KANNOSUKE
SPINY OYSTER BAR
ABC Hall
FUKUSHIMA
Dojima-gawa

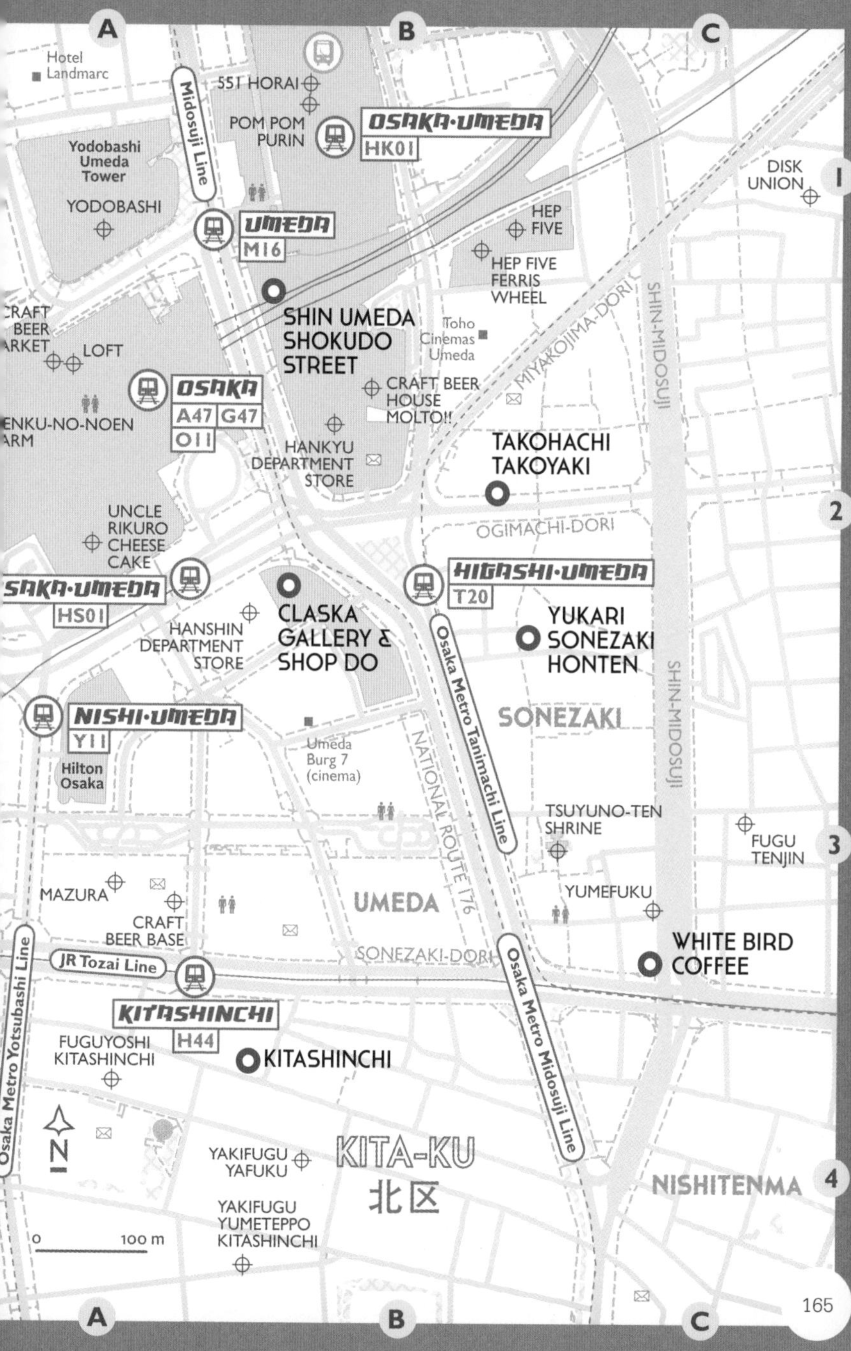
A
B
C
Hotel Landmarc
551 HORAI
POM POM PURIN
OSAKA-UMEDA
HK01
Midosuji Line
Yodobashi Umeda Tower
YODOBASHI
UMEDA
M16
DISK UNION
HEP FIVE
HEP FIVE FERRIS WHEEL
SHIN UMEDA SHOKUDO STREET
Toho Cinemas Umeda
LOFT
OSAKA
A47
G47
O11
CRAFT BEER HOUSE MOLTO!!
MIYAKOJIMA-DORI
SHIN-MIDOSUJI
HANKYU DEPARTMENT STORE
TAKOHACHI TAKOYAKI
UNCLE RIKURO CHEESE CAKE
OGIMACHI-DORI
HIGASHI-UMEDA
T20
HS01
CLASKA GALLERY & SHOP DO
YUKARI SONEZAKI HONTEN
HANSHIN DEPARTMENT STORE
Osaka Metro Tanimachi Line
NISHI-UMEDA
Y11
SONEZAKI
Hilton Osaka
Umeda Burg 7 (cinema)
NATIONAL ROUTE 176
TSUYUNO-TEN SHRINE
FUGU TENJIN
MAZURA
CRAFT BEER BASE
UMEDA
YUMEFUKU
WHITE BIRD COFFEE
SONEZAKI-DORI
JR Tozai Line
Osaka Metro Yotsubashi Line
KITASHINCHI
H44
Osaka Metro Midosuji Line
FUGUYOSHI KITASHINCHI
KITASHINCHI
N
YAKIFUGU YAFUKU
KITA-KU
北区
NISHITENMA
YAKIFUGU YUMETEPPO KITASHINCHI
0
100 m
1
2
3
4

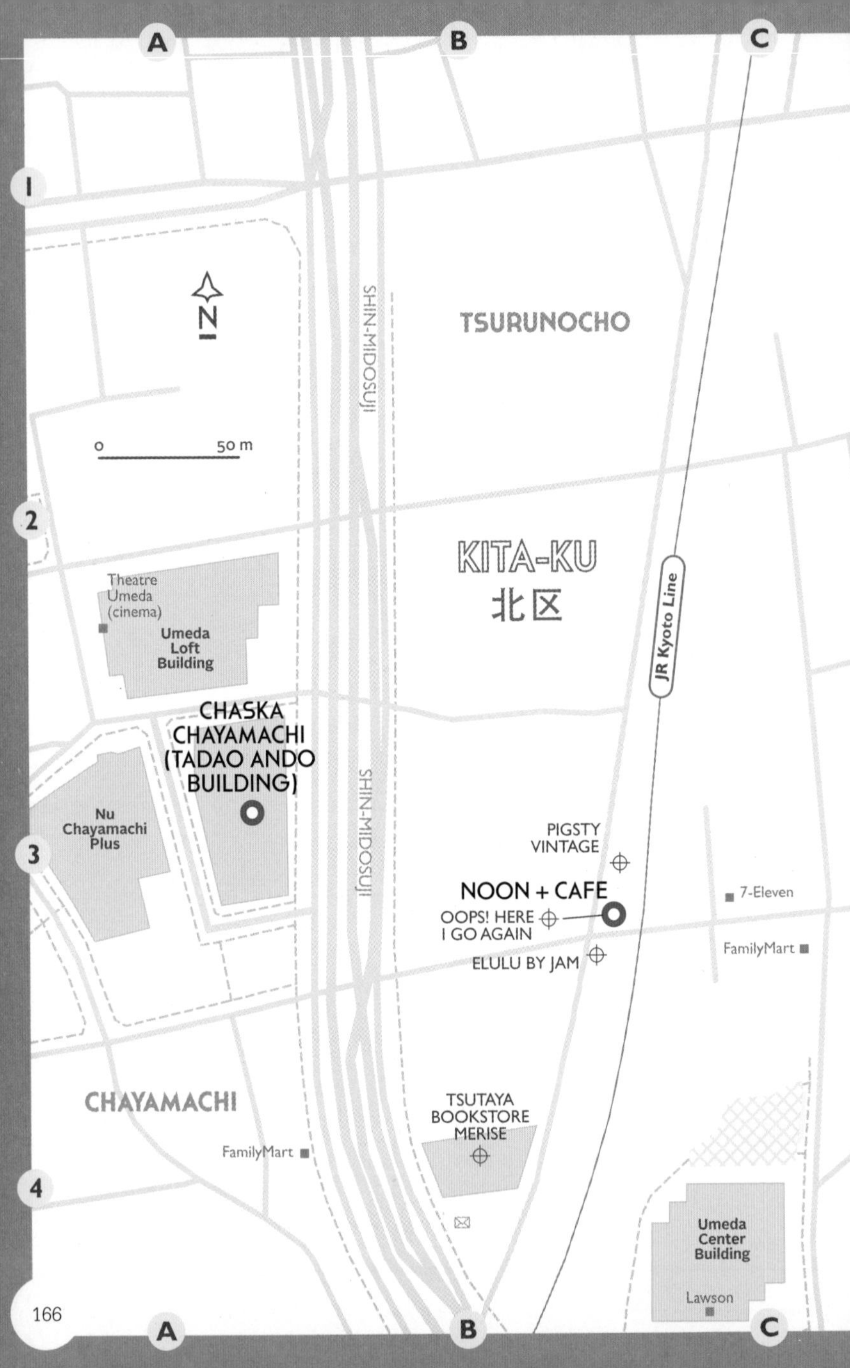
A
B
C
1
2
3
4
N
0
50 m
TSURUNOCHO
SHIN-MIDOSUJI
KITA-KU
北区
JR Kyoto Line
Theatre
Umeda
(cinema)
Umeda
Loft
Building
CHASKA
CHAYAMACHI
(TADAO ANDO
BUILDING)
Nu
Chayamachi
Plus
PIGSTY
VINTAGE
NOON + CAFE
OOPS! HERE
I GO AGAIN
ELULU BY JAM
7-Eleven
FamilyMart
CHAYAMACHI
TSUTAYA
BOOKSTORE
MERISE
FamilyMart
Umeda
Center
Building
Lawson

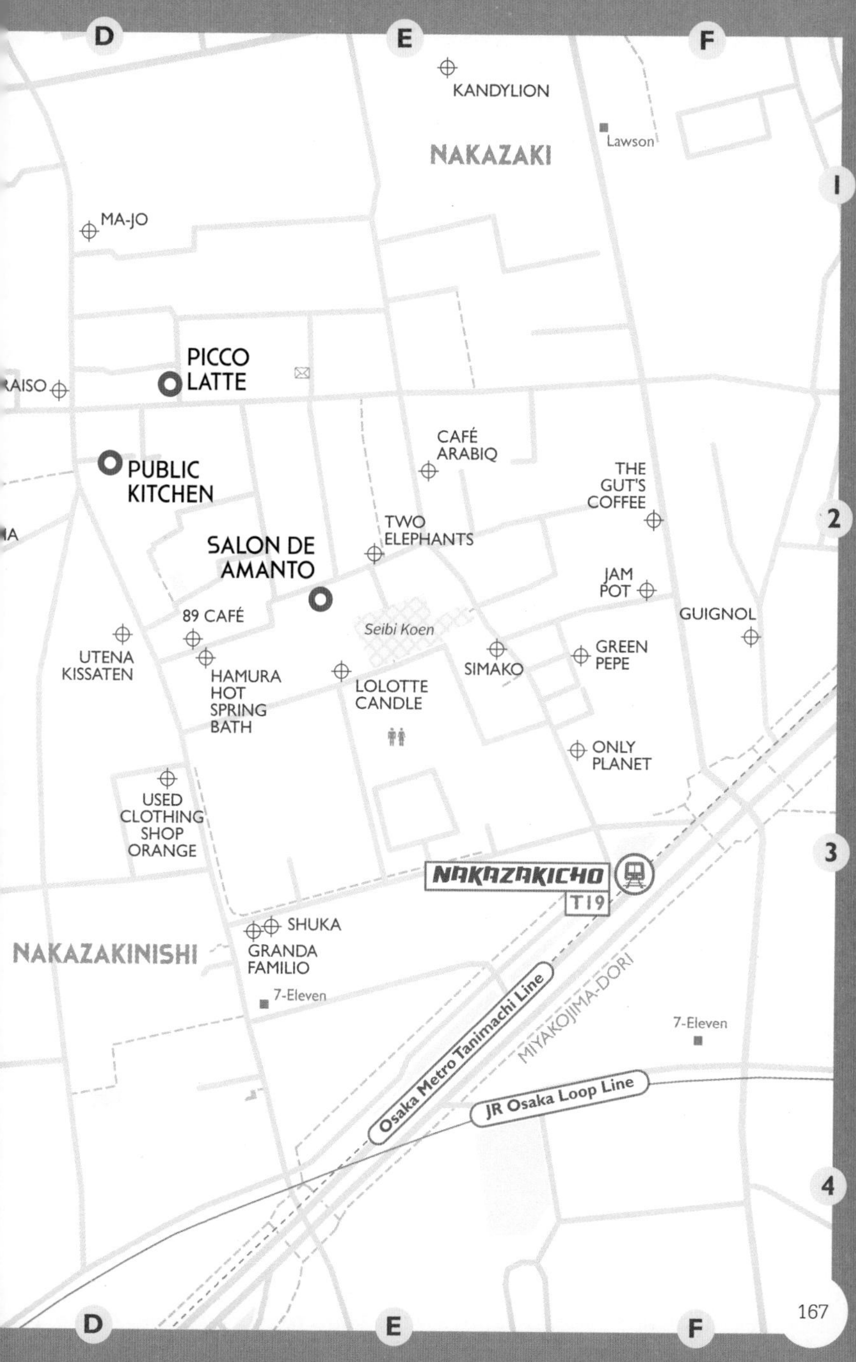
D
E
F
KANDYLION
Lawson
NAKAZAKI
I
MA-JO
PICCO
LATTE
RAISO
PUBLIC
KITCHEN
CAFÉ
ARABIQ
THE
GUT'S
COFFEE
2
TWO
ELEPHANTS
SALON DE
AMANTO
JAM
POT
GUIGNOL
89 CAFÉ
Seibi Koen
UTENA
KISSATEN
HAMURA
HOT
SPRING
BATH
LOLOTTE
CANDLE
SIMAKO
GREEN
PEPE
ONLY
PLANET
USED
CLOTHING
SHOP
ORANGE
3
NAKAZAKICHO
T19
SHUKA
GRANDA
FAMILIO
NAKAZAKINISHI
7-Eleven
Osaka Metro Tanimachi Line
MIYAKOJIMA-DORI
7-Eleven
JR Osaka Loop Line
4
D
E
F

TENJIMBASHISUJI ROKUCHOME
K11 T18
MIYAKOJIMADORI
Osaka Metro Tanimachi Line
OSAKA MUSEUM OF HOUSING AND LIVING
McDonald's
Lawson
FamilyMart
TENJINBASHI
TENJINBASHI-SUJI SHOPPING MALL
OSAKA TAKATSUKI KYOTO LINE
Osaka Metro Sakaisuji Line
KANEICHO
KITA-KU
北区
7-Eleven
TENJINBASHI-SUJI SHOPPING STREET
IKEDACHO
HARUKOMA HONTEN SUSHI
CHOCHIN DORI
YOIDORE KUJIRA
ORB
KOBACHIYA BAR
URA-TENMA
BEER BELLY TENMA
NIKUZUSHI
PULALA TENMA
N
0
50
A
B
C
1
2
3
4

A
B
C
MINAMI-MORIMACHI
K13 T21
OSAKATEMMANGU
H43
Osaka Metro Sakaisuji Line
SONEZAKI-DORI
JR Tozai Line
FamilyMart
Osaka Metro Tanimachi Line
FamilyMart
FamilyMart
SONEZAKI-DORI
TEORIYA
HIGASHITENMA
1
7-Eleven
OSAKA TENMANGU SHRINE
KAGURADEN
0 50 m
TENJINBASHISUJI
TENJINBASHI-SUJI SHOPPING MALL
TENMA
Lawson
2
KITA-KU
北区
N
FamilyMart
TOKIONA
Takigawa Koen
TENJINBASHI
TENJINBASHISUJI
3
7-Eleven
JTRRD
YONAGADOU
SECOND BANANA
RJ CAFÉ
Dojima-gawa
Minami-temma Koen
Tenjinbashi (Tenjin Bridge)
4
Nakanoshima Koen
Fountain
Okawa
A
B
C

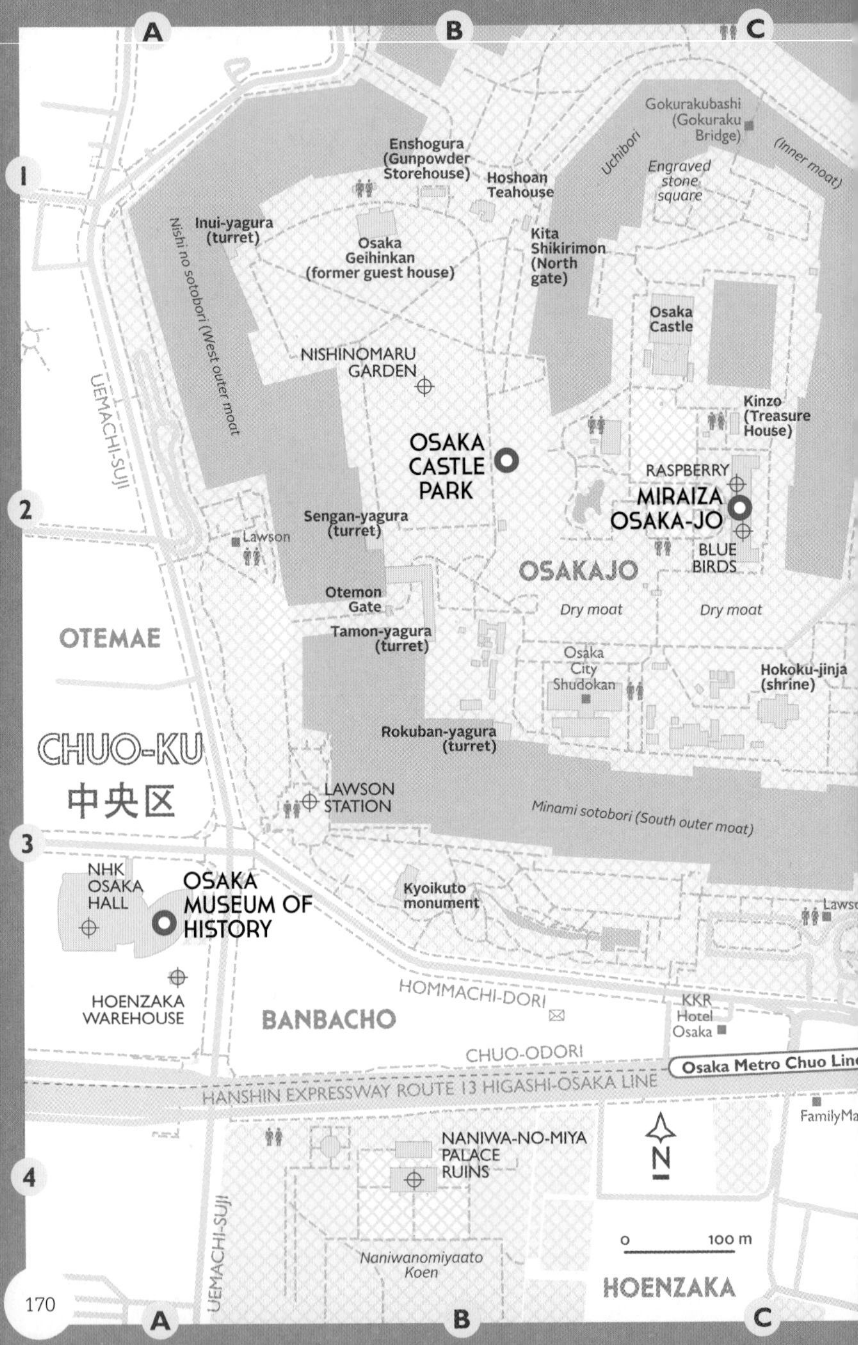

A
B
C
1
2
3
4
Gokurakubashi
(Gokuraku
Bridge)
(Inner moat)
Uchibori
Engraved
stone
square
Enshogura
(Gunpowder
Storehouse)
Hoshoan
Teahouse
Inui-yagura
(turret)
Nishi no sotobori (West outer moat
Osaka
Geihinkan
(former guest house)
Kita
Shikirimon
(North
gate)
Osaka
Castle
NISHINOMARU
GARDEN
UEMACHI-SUJI
Kinzo
(Treasure
House)
OSAKA
CASTLE
PARK
RASPBERRY
MIRAIZA
OSAKA-JO
BLUE
BIRDS
Sengan-yagura
(turret)
Lawson
OSAKAJO
Otemon
Gate
Dry moat
Dry moat
OTEMAE
Tamon-yagura
(turret)
Osaka
City
Shudokan
Hokoku-jinja
(shrine)
CHUO-KU
中央区
Rokuban-yagura
(turret)
LAWSON
STATION
Minami sotobori (South outer moat)
NHK
OSAKA
HALL
OSAKA
MUSEUM OF
HISTORY
Kyoikuto
monument
Lawso
HOENZAKA
WAREHOUSE
HOMMACHI-DORI
BANBACHO
KKR
Hotel
Osaka
CHUO-ODORI
Osaka Metro Chuo Line
HANSHIN EXPRESSWAY ROUTE 13 HIGASHI-OSAKA LINE
FamilyMa
NANIWA-NO-MIYA
PALACE
RUINS
N
0
100 m
UEMACHI-SUJI
Naniwanomiyaato
Koen
HOENZAKA

A
B
C
MORINOMIYA
O06
MORINOMIYACHUO
0
100 m
1
N
HIGASHINARI-KU
東成区
2
MABATAKI
CHUO-KU
中央区
JR Osaka Loop Line
NAKAMICHI
3
Hirano-gawa
Chudoyasaka-jinja
(Shinto shrine)
TAMATSUKURI
4
awson
NAGAHORI-DORI
7-Eleven
A
B
C

A
B
C
1
2
3
4
MINATOMACHI OCAT
JR NAMBA
Q17
OSAKA NAMBA
A01
HS41
NAMBA
S16
Y15
M20
Lawson
FamilyMart
JR Yamatoji Line
7-Eleven
FamilyMart
Osaka Metro Yotsubashi Line
Tetsugenji (Buddhist temple)
MINATOMACHI
0
100 m
YOTSUBASHI-KIN
NATIONAL ROUTE 25
Osaka Metro Midosuji Line
FamilyMart
N
NANBANAKA
Naniwa Koen
FamilyMart
MOTOMACHI
FamilyMart
EDION Arena Osaka
NAMBA YASAKA SHRINE
Toyoko Inn Osaka Nanba
Naniwa Sports Centre
Nanbanaka Koen
NANIWA-KU
浪速区
7-Eleven
NATIONAL ROUTE 25
7-Eleven
FamilyMart
Kamomecho Koen
SHIKITSUHIGASHI

D
E
F
Osaka Metro Sennichimae Line
Kintetsu Nara Line
NIPPOMBASHI
K17 S17
Cemetery
KINTETSU-NIPPOMBASHI
A02
1
IBUKI
COFFEE
KUROMON
Osaka Metro Sakaisuji Line
Toho
Cinemas
Lawson
MISONO
BUILDING
Namba
Plaza
Hotel
Namba
Grand
Kagetsu
(theatre)
KUROMON
ICHIBA
MARKET
YES
Namba
Building
EVA
EVAM
URA-NAMBA
NIPPONBASHI
2
Swissotel
Nankai Osaka
SAKAISUJI
Kuromon
Koen
SENNICHIMAE
DOGUYASUJI
SHOTENGAI
7-Eleven
NAMBA
NK01
CHUO-KU
中央区
Lawson
Namba City
Nankai
(shopping
centre)
7-Eleven
NARUTO
TAIYAKI
HOMPO
OTARODO
FamilyMart
Lawson
YELLOW
SUBMARINE
3
SUPER
POTATO
REPTILE
CAFE
ROCK
STAR
FamilyMart
Nipponbashi
Koen
Namba
Parks
7-Eleven
OTA
ROAD
Namba
Parks
Cinema
HERO
GANGU
ANIMATE
FamilyMart
Lawson
Lawson
Nankai Main Line
7-Eleven
SAKAISUJI
4
Nipponbashi
Crystal Hotel
OTARODO
JOSHIN SUPER
KIDS LAND
DEN DEN
TOWN
D
E
F

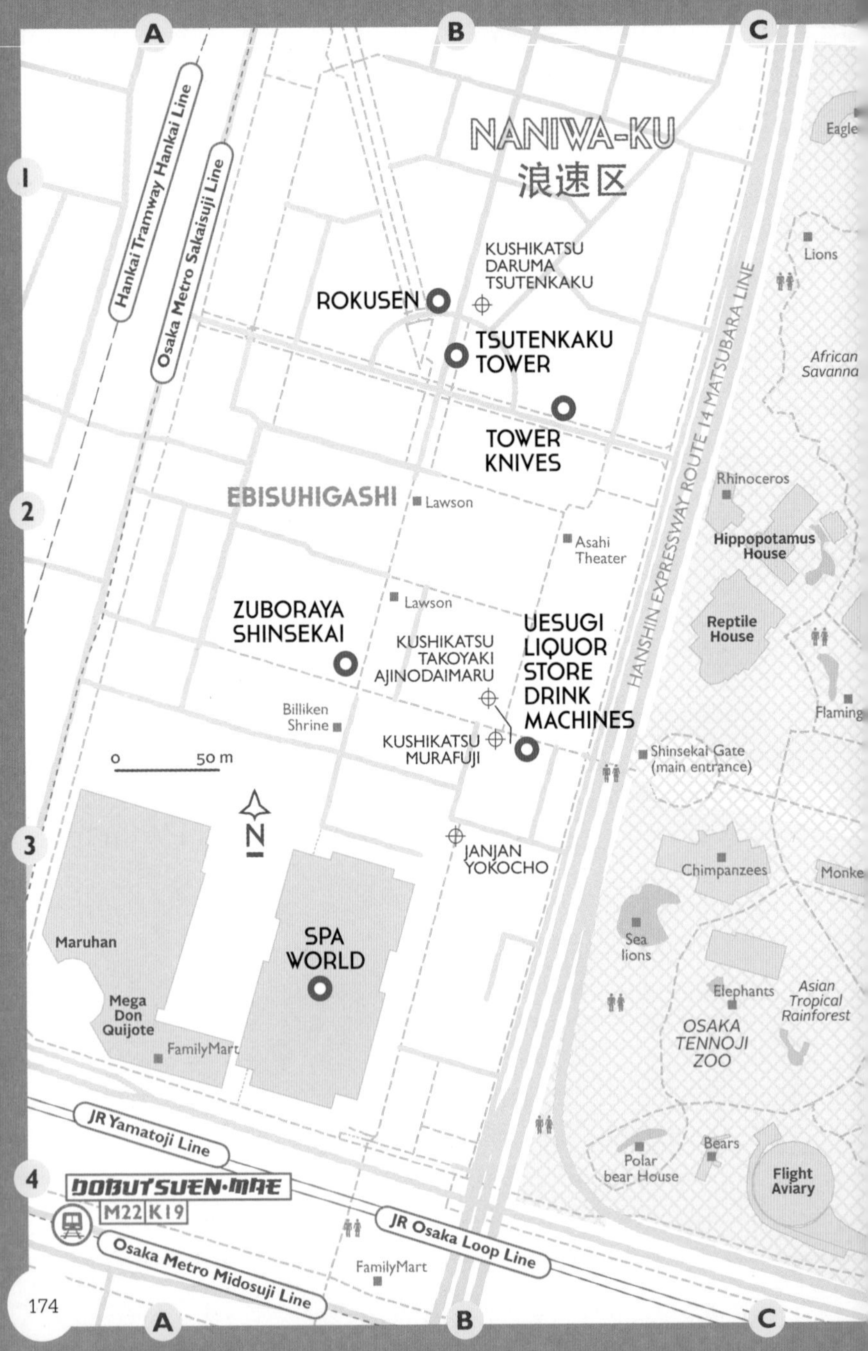

A
B
C
1
2
3
4
NANIWA-KU
浪速区
Hankai Tramway Hankai Line
Osaka Metro Sakaisuji Line
HANSHIN EXPRESSWAY ROUTE 14 MATSUBARA LINE
KUSHIKATSU DARUMA TSUTENKAKU
ROKUSEN
TSUTENKAKU TOWER
TOWER KNIVES
EBISUHIGASHI
Lawson
Asahi Theater
Lawson
ZUBORAYA SHINSEKAI
KUSHIKATSU TAKOYAKI AJINODAIMARU
UESUGI LIQUOR STORE DRINK MACHINES
Billiken Shrine
KUSHIKATSU MURAFUJI
Shinsekai Gate (main entrance)
0 50 m
N
JANJAN YOKOCHO
SPA WORLD
Maruhan
Mega Don Quijote
FamilyMart
JR Yamatoji Line
DOBUTSUEN-MAE
M22 K19
JR Osaka Loop Line
Osaka Metro Midosuji Line
FamilyMart
Eagle
Lions
African Savanna
Rhinoceros
Hippopotamus House
Reptile House
Flaming
Chimpanzees
Monke
Sea lions
Elephants
Asian Tropical Rainforest
OSAKA TENNOJI ZOO
Polar bear House
Bears
Flight Aviary

A
B
C
SHITANNOJI·MAE YUHIGAOKA
T26
TENNOJI-KU
天王寺区
UEMACHI-SUJI
YUHIGAOKACHO
Osaka Metro Tanimachi Line
FamilyMart
Oe-jinja (Shinto shrine)
KATSUYAMA DORI
REININCHO
TANIMACHI-SUJI
Shitennoji Cemetery
GOKURAKUJODO GARDEN
Eirei-do Shrine
Toko-in Shrine
Daikoku-do Shrine
N
Rokujireisando Prayer Hall
SHITENNOJI
0
100 m
SHITENNOJI TEMPLE
BENZAITEN SHRINE
Kondo (main hall)
CHUSHIN GARAN
Saijumon
Chumon (middle gate)
NATIONAL ROUTE 25
SHITENNOJI FLEA MARKET
Lawson
DAIDO
FamilyMart
Tennoji Park
Horikoshi-jinja (Shinto shrine)
Kawazoko-ike
FamilyMart
1
2
3
4

INDEX

ABOUT THE AUTHORS

Steve and Michelle are Japan obsessives. It's their home away from home 3+ months of the year. This is their third Japan book in the Pocket Precinct series (Tokyo Pocket Precincts and Kyoto Pocket Precincts have been translated into Korean and German). They have also authored a guide to hot springs bathing, Onsen of Japan (translated into three languages), and a larger volume on Tokyo.

At home in Melbourne, Michelle is an award-winning book designer and illustrator and Steve is an indie radio DJ.

ACKNOWLEDGEMENTS

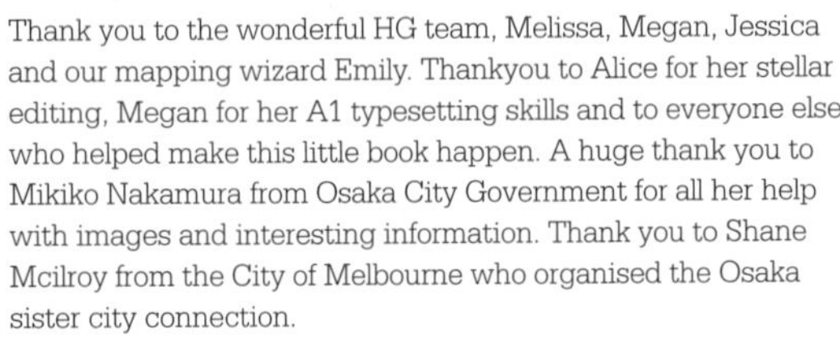

Thank you to the wonderful HG team, Melissa, Megan, Jessica and our mapping wizard Emily. Thankyou to Alice for her stellar editing, Megan for her A1 typesetting skills and to everyone else who helped make this little book happen. A huge thank you to Mikiko Nakamura from Osaka City Government for all her help with images and interesting information. Thank you to Shane Mcilroy from the City of Melbourne who organised the Osaka sister city connection.

Thank-you to our wonderful friends Hiki and Coco for helping us with Japanese translations and research and for their friendship. And to Jane Ormond for her last minute photo genius.

PHOTO CREDITS

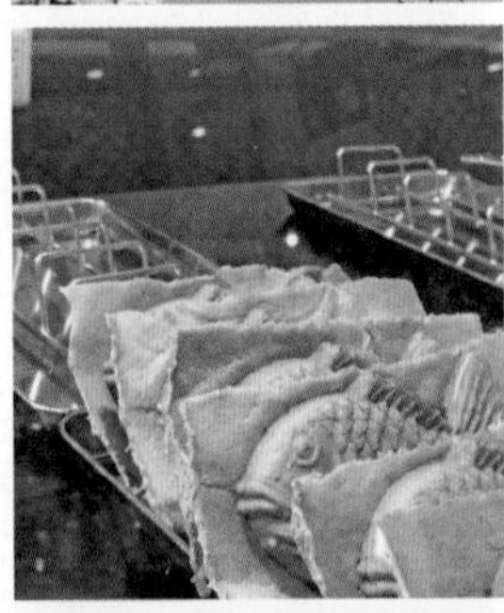

All images © Michelle Mackintosh and Steve Wide, except for the following:

p.2 bottom ©Cody Chan Unsplash, 19 middle ©Esther Tuttle Unsplash, 22 ©Pico Latte, 26 ©Ignis, cc-by-sa-3.0-migrated, Wikicommons, 27 top ©Inoue-hiro, cc-by-sa-3.0 Wikicommons, 28 ©Jane Ormond, 29 ©Shibakawa Building, "Yoshiro masuda" and "Chishima real estate co.,Ltd." 30-31 ©Graf, 50 bottom ©Babymetal by Sven Mandel Unsplash, 64 ©Yuki Museum of Art, 65 images ©Kenpei, Wikicommons, 85 top ©NY066 at wts wikivoyage, middle ©Richard Enjoymylife! cc-by-sa-2.0 Wikicommons, 89 top & middle ©Cafe Ori Ori, 93 bottom ©Osaka Convention & Tourism Bureau, 94 ©Mabataki, 100 ©bottom, 101-102 ©Osaka Convention & Tourism Bureau, 105 ©Yonagadou, 112-113 ©SPA WORLD, 114 middle ©Hotel Public Jam, 115 and top 126 ©Tower Knives, 121©Hankyu Corporation, 122 top ©Motokoka CC-BY-SA-4.0 & bottom ©Ujigis CC-BY-SA-4.0 Wikicommons, 123 top ©Kirakirameister, cc-by-sa-3.0 Wikicommons, bottom ©Bob Jansen Unsplash, 124 ©Osaka Convention & Tourism Bureau, 125 ©Shiba Ryotaro Memorial Museum, 126 top ©Tower Knives bottom ©Laitche CC-BY-SA-4.0, Wikicommons, 127 top ©Saigen Jiro, bottom ©Yanajin33, cc-by-sa-3.0 Wikicommons, 129 top ©chee.hong cc-by-2.0 Wikicommons, bottom ©Matt Chris Pua Unsplash, 130 ©KenpeI cc-by-sa-3.0-migrated Wikicommons, 131 top ©Alamy, 131 bottom ©yoppy cc-by-2.0 Wikicommons

Published in 2020 by Hardie Grant Travel, a division of Hardie Grant Publishing

Hardie Grant Travel (Melbourne)
Building 1, 658 Church Street
Richmond, Victoria 3121

Hardie Grant Travel (Sydney)
Level 7, 45 Jones Street
Ultimo, NSW 2007

www.hardiegrant.com/au/travel

The maps in this publication incorporate data from:

© OpenStreetMap contributors
OpenStreetMap is made available under the Open Data Commons Open Database License (ODbL) by the OpenStreetMap Foundation (OSMF): http://opendatacommons.org/licenses/odbl/1.0/. Any rights in individual contents of the database are licensed under the Database Contents License: http://opendatacommons.org/licenses/dbcl/1.0/
Data extracts via Geofabrik GmbH https://www.geofabrik.de
© National Land Information Division, National Spatial Planning and Regional Policy Bureau, MILT of Japan

A catalogue record for this book is available from the National Library of Australia

Osaka Pocket Precincts
ISBN 9781741176834

10 9 8 7 6 5 4 3 2 1

Publisher
Melissa Kayser

Project editor
Megan Cuthbert

Editor
Alice Barker

Proofreader
Jessica Smith

Cartographic research
Claire Johnston

Cartography
Emily Maffei

Design
Michelle Mackintosh

Typesetting
Megan Ellis

Index
Max McMaster

Prepress
Megan Ellis and Splitting Image Colour Studio

Printed in Singapore by 1010 Printing International Limited

Disclaimer: While every care is taken to ensure the accuracy of the data within this product, the owners of the data do not make any representations or warranties about its accuracy, reliability, completeness or suitability for any particular purpose and, to the extent permitted by law, the owners of the data disclaim all responsibility and all liability (including without limitation, liability in negligence) for all expenses, losses, damages (including indirect or consequential damages) and costs which might be incurred as a result of the data being inaccurate or incomplete in any way and for any reason.

Publisher's Disclaimers: The publisher cannot accept responsibility for any errors or omissions. The representation on the maps of any road or track is not necessarily evidence of public right of way. The publisher cannot be held responsible for any injury, loss or damage incurred during travel. It is vital to research any proposed trip thoroughly and seek the advice of relevant state and travel organisations before you leave.

Publisher's Note: Every effort has been made to ensure that the information in this book is accurate at the time of going to press. The publisher welcomes information and suggestions for correction or improvement.

POCKET PRECINCTS SERIES

COLLECT THE SET!

Curated guidebooks offering the best cultural, eating and drinking spots to experience the city as the locals do. Each guidebook includes detailed maps at the back and a field trip section encouraging you to venture further afield.

These compact guides are perfect for slipping into your back pocket before you head out on your next adventure.

COMING SOON

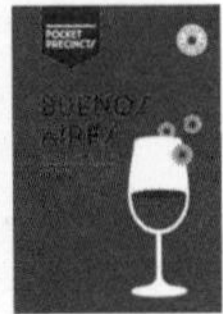